TEST PREP 2018

Study & Prepare

Pass your test and know what is essential to safely operate an unmanned aircraft—from the most trusted source in aviation training

Remote Pilot

READER TIP:
The FAA Knowledge Exam Questions can change throughout the year. Stay current with test changes; sign up for ASA's free email update service at www.asa2fly.com/testupdate

Aviation Supplies & Academics, Inc.
Newcastle, Washington

2018 Remote Pilot Test Prep

Aviation Supplies & Academics, Inc.
7005 132nd Place SE
Newcastle, Washington 98059-3153
425.235.1500
www.asa2fly.com

Important: This Test Prep should be sold with and used in conjunction with Airman Knowledge Testing Supplement for Sport Pilot, Recreational Pilot, and Private Pilot (FAA-CT-8080-2G). ASA reprints the FAA test figures and legends within this government document, and it is also sold separately and available from aviation retailers nationwide. Order #ASA-CT-8080-2G.

Cover photo: Courtesy Freefly Systems Inc.
www.freeflysystems.com

ASA-TP-UAS-18
ISBN   978-1-61954-559-5

Printed in the United States of America

2018   2017   5   4   3   2   1

Stay informed of aviation industry happenings

Website	www.asa2fly.com
Updates	www.asa2fly.com/testupdate
Twitter	www.twitter.com/asa2fly
Facebook	www.facebook.com/asa2fly
Blog	www.learntoflyblog.com

About the Contributors

Jackie Spanitz

Director of Curriculum Development
Aviation Supplies & Academics, Inc.

As Director of Curriculum Development for Aviation Supplies & Academics, Jackie Spanitz oversees maintenance and development of more than 750 titles and pilot supplies in the ASA product line. Ms. Spanitz has worked with airman training and testing for more than 20 years, including participation in the ACS development committees. Jackie holds a Bachelor degree in aviation technology from Western Michigan University, a Masters degree from Embry Riddle Aeronautical University, and Instructor and Commercial Pilot certificates. She is the author of *Guide to the Flight Review*, and the technical editor for ASA's *Test Prep* and *FAR/AIM* series.

David Ison, Ph.D.

Assistant Professor, College of Aeronautics
Embry-Riddle Aeronautical University-Worldwide

Dr. David Ison is an Assistant Professor of Aeronautics and Research Chair for the College of Aeronautics, ERAU-Worldwide. He holds a Ph.D. in Educational Studies/Higher Education Leadership/Aviation Higher Education from the University of Nebraska Lincoln, a Master's of Aeronautical Science from ERAU, and a B.S. in Aviation Management from Auburn University. He is a co-author of the comprehensive textbook *Small Unmanned Aircraft Systems Guide: Exploring Designs, Operations, Regulations, and Economics.*

About ASA: Aviation Supplies & Academics, Inc. (ASA) is an industry leader in the development and sale of aviation supplies and publications for pilots, flight instructors, flight engineers, air traffic controllers, flight attendants, and aviation maintenance technicians. We manufacture and publish more than 700 products, and have been providing trusted and reliable training materials to the aviation industry for more than 75 years. Aviators are invited to visit **www.asa2fly.com** for a free copy of our catalog.

Contents

Continued

Chapter 5 **Operations**

Preface

Welcome to ASA's Test Prep Series. ASA's test books have been helping pilots prepare for the FAA Knowledge Tests for more than 60 years with great success. We are confident that with proper use of this book, you will score very well on the Remote Pilot certificate test for the small unmanned aircraft system (sUAS) rating.

Begin your studies with a classroom or home-study ground school course, which will involve reading a textbook to gain the aeronautical knowledge required to earn your Remote Pilot certificate. Visit the dedicated Reader Resource webpage for this Test Prep (**www.asa2fly.com/reader/TPUAS**) and become familiar with the FAA guidance materials available for this certification exam. Conclude your studies by reviewing the Chapter Text in this book which precedes each question section. Read the question, select your choice for the correct answer, then read the explanation. Use the references that conclude each explanation to identify additional resources if you need further study of a subject. Upon completion of your studies, take practice tests at **www.prepware.com** (see inside front cover for your free account).

The FAA Unmanned Aircraft Systems questions have been arranged into chapters based on subject matter. Topical study, in which similar material is covered under a common subject heading, promotes better understanding, aids recall, and thus provides a more efficient study guide.

It is important to answer every question assigned on your FAA Knowledge Test. If in their ongoing review, the FAA authors decide a question has no correct answer, is no longer applicable, or is otherwise defective, your answer will be marked correct no matter which one you chose. However, you will not be given the automatic credit unless you have marked an answer. Unlike some other exams you may have taken, there is no penalty for "guessing" in this instance.

The FAA exams are "closed tests" which means the exact database of questions is not available to the public. The question and answer choices in this book are based on our extensive history and experience with the FAA testing process. You might see similar although not exactly the same questions on your official FAA exam. Answer stems may be rearranged from the A, B, C order you see in this book. Therefore, be careful to fully understand the intent of each question and corresponding answer while studying, rather than memorize the A, B, C answer. You may be asked a question that has unfamiliar wording; studying and understanding the information in this book and the associated references will give you the tools to answer question variations with confidence.

If your study leads you to question an answer choice, we recommend you seek the assistance of a local instructor. We welcome your questions, recommendations or concerns:

Aviation Supplies & Academics, Inc.
7005 132nd Place SE
Newcastle, WA 98059-3153
Voice: 425.235.1500   Fax: 425.235.0128
Email: cfi@asa2fly.com   Website: www.asa2fly.com

The FAA appreciates testing experience feedback. You can contact the branch responsible for the FAA Knowledge Exams at:

Federal Aviation Administration
AFS-630, Airman Testing Standards Branch
PO Box 25082
Oklahoma City, OK 73125
Email: afs630comments@faa.gov

Updates and Practice Tests

Free Test Updates for the One-Year Life Cycle of Test Prep Books

The FAA rolls out new tests as needed throughout the year; this typically happens in June, October, and February. The FAA exams are "closed tests" which means the exact database of questions is not available to the public. ASA combines more than 60 years of experience with expertise in airman training and certification tests to prepare the most effective test preparation materials available in the industry.

You can feel confident you will be prepared for your FAA Knowledge Exam by using the ASA Test Preps. ASA keeps abreast of changes to the tests. These changes are then posted on the ASA website as a Test Update.

Visit the ASA website before taking your test to be certain you have the most current information, including the reader resource page: **www.asa2fly.com/reader/TPUAS**. Additionally, sign up for ASA's free email Update service. We will then send you an email notification if there is a change to the test you are preparing for so you can review the Update for revised and/or new test information.

www.asa2fly.com/testupdate

We invite your feedback. After you take your official FAA exam, let us know how you did. Were you prepared? Did the ASA products meet your needs and exceed your expectations? We want to continue to improve these products to ensure applicants are prepared, and become safe aviators. Send feedback to: **cfi@asa2fly.com**

Description of the Test

The knowledge test is an important part of the airman certification process. Applicants who do not meet the requirements in 14 CFR §107.61 (d)(1), must pass the knowledge test before preparing an application for a Remote Pilot Certificate with a Small UAS Rating.

The knowledge test consists of objective, multiple-choice questions. There is a single correct response for each test question. Each test question is independent of other questions. A correct response to one question does not depend upon, or influence, the correct response to another.

Test Code	Test Name	Number of Questions	Min. Age	Allotted Time (hrs)
UAG	Unmanned Aircraft General—Small	60	14	2.0

The 60-question FAA UAG Knowledge Exam consists of the following subject composition:

UAS Topics	Percentage of Items on Test
I. Regulations	15–25%
II. Airspace & Requirements	8–15%
III. Weather	11–16%
IV. Loading and Performance	7–11%
V. Operations	13–18%

Before starting the actual test, the testing center will provide an opportunity to practice navigating through the test. This practice or tutorial session may include sample questions to familiarize the applicant with the look and feel of the software, such as selecting an answer, marking a question for later review, monitoring time remaining for the test, and other features of the testing software.

FAA Knowledge Test Question Coding

The FAA publishes an Airman Certification Standard (ACS) to detail the knowledge requirements needed to earn a Remote Pilot certificate; this FAA document can be viewed at **www.asa2fly.com/reader/TPUAS**. Each task in the ACS includes an ACS code. This ACS code will soon be displayed on the airman test report to indicate what Task element was proven deficient on the Knowledge Exam. The ACS coding consists of four elements. This code is deciphered as follows:

UA.I.B.K10

UA—Applicable ACS (Unmanned Aircraft Systems)

I—Area of Operation (Regulations)

B—Task (Operating Rules)

K10—Task element (Knowledge 10: Visual line of sight aircraft operations.)

Knowledge test questions are mapped to the ACS codes, which will soon replace the system of "Learning Statement Codes." After this transition occurs, the Airman Knowledge Test Report (AKTR) will list an ACS code that correlates to a specific element for a given Area of Operation and Task.

To obtain a copy of the LSC that will be found on the AKTR, please refer to **www.faa.gov**. To review questions associated with the LSC codes on your AKTR refer to Appendix B: Learning Statement Code and Question Number.

Knowledge Test Registration

The FAA authorizes hundreds of knowledge testing center locations that offer a full range of airman knowledge tests. For information on authorized testing centers and to register for the knowledge test, contact one of the providers listed at **https://www.faa.gov/training_testing/testing/media/test_centers.pdf**.

When you contact a knowledge testing center to register for a test, be prepared to select a test date, choose a testing center, and make financial arrangements for test payment when you call. You may register for test(s) several weeks in advance, and you may cancel in accordance with the testing center's cancellation policy.

The following airman knowledge testing (AKT) organization designation authorization (ODA) holders are authorized to give FAA knowledge tests. This list should be helpful to register for a test or if you simply want more information.

Computer Assisted Testing Service (CATS)
Applicant inquiry and test registration: 800-947-4228 or 650-259-8550
www.catstest.com

PSI Computer Testing
Applicant inquiry and test registration: 800-211-2753 or 360-896-9111
www.psiexams.com

Knowledge Test Requirements

To verify your eligibility to take the knowledge test, you must meet the following in accordance with the requirements of Advisory Circular (AC) 107-2:

1. You must be at least 14 years of age to take the knowledge test.

2. You must provide proper identification which contains —

   a. Photograph;

   b. Signature;

   c. Date of birth;

   d. If the permanent mailing address is a post office box number, then you must provide a current government-issued address.

A list of acceptable documents used to provide proper identification can be found in AC 61-65, Certification: Pilots and Flight and Ground Instructors.

Achieving a score of 70% or better is required to be considered as satisfactorily passing the knowledge test for a Remote Pilot Certificate with a Small UAS Rating.

Acceptable Materials

The applicant may use the following aids, reference materials, and test materials, as long as the material does not include actual test questions or answers.

Acceptable Materials	Unacceptable Materials	Notes
Supplement book provided by proctor.	Written materials that are handwritten, printed, or electronic.	Testing centers may provide calculators and/or deny the use of personal calculators.
All models of aviation-oriented calculators or small electronic calculators that perform only arithmetic functions.	Electronic calculators incorporating permanent or continuous type memory circuits without erasure capability.	Unit Member (proctor) may prohibit the use of your calculator if he or she is unable to determine the calculator's erasure capability.
Calculators with simple programmable memories, which allow addition to, subtraction from, or retrieval of one number from the memory; or simple functions, such as square root and percentages.	Magnetic cards, magnetic tapes, modules, computer chips, or any other device upon which pre-written programs or information related to the test can be stored and retrieved.	Printouts of data must be surrendered at the completion of the test if the calculator incorporates this design feature.
Scales, straight-edges, protractors, plotters, navigation computers, blank log sheets, holding pattern entry aids, and electronic or mechanical calculators that are directly related to the test.	Dictionaries.	Before, and upon completion of the test, while in the presence of the Unit Member, actuate the ON/OFF switch or RESET button, and perform any other function that ensures erasure of any data stored in memory circuits.
Manufacturer's permanently inscribed instructions on the front and back of such aids, such as formulas, conversions, regulations, signals, weather data, holding pattern diagrams, frequencies, weight and balance formulas, and ATC procedures.	Any booklet or manual containing instructions related to use of test aids.	Unit Member makes the final determination regarding aids, reference materials, and test materials.

Retesting Procedure

14 CFR §107.71 specifies that an applicant who fails the knowledge test may not retake the knowledge test for 14 calendar days from the date of the previous failure.

An applicant retesting after failure is required to submit the applicable AKTR indicating failure to the testing center prior to retesting.

No instructor endorsement or other form of written authorization is required to retest after failure. The original failed AKTR must be retained by the proctor and attached to the applicable daily log.

Note: If the testing center is approved for electronic filing, the proctor must initial the AKTR within the embossed seal, file the AKTR IAW their AKT ODA Holder's Procedures Manual, and destroy the AKTR. The proctor must verify the original failed AKTR has been successfully captured and stored prior to destruction. If the applicant no longer possesses the AKTR, he or she may request a duplicate replacement issued by AFS-760.

Cheating or Other Unauthorized Conduct

To avoid test compromise, computer testing centers must follow strict security procedures established by the FAA and described in FAA Order 8080.6, Conduct of Airman Knowledge Tests. The FAA has directed testing centers to terminate a test at any time a test unit member suspects that a cheating incident has occurred.

The FAA will investigate and, if the agency determines that cheating or unauthorized conduct has occurred, any airman certificate or rating you hold may be revoked. You will also be prohibited from applying for or taking any test for a certificate or rating under 14 CFR §107.69 for a period of one year.

Testing Procedures for Applicants Requesting Special Accommodations

An applicant with learning or reading disability may request approval from AFS-630 through the local Flight Standards District Office (FSDO) or International Field Office/International Field Unit (IFO/IFU) to take airman knowledge test using one of the three options listed below, in preferential order:

1. Use current testing facilities and procedures whenever possible.
2. Use a self-contained, electronic device which pronounces and displays typed-in words, such as the Franklin Speaking Wordmaster®) to facilitate the testing process.
3. Request the proctor's assistance in reading specific words or terms from the test questions and/or supplement book. To prevent compromising the testing process, the proctor must be an individual with no aviation background or expertise. The proctor may provide reading assistance only (i.e., no explanation of words or terms). When an applicant requests this option, the applicant must contact the AFS-630 for assistance in selecting the test site and assisting the proctor.

Note: The device should consist of an electronic thesaurus that audibly pronounces typed-in words and presents them on a display screen. The device should also have a built-in headphone jack in order to avoid disturbing others during testing.

Test Report

Immediately upon completion of the knowledge test, you will receive a printed AKTR documenting the score with the testing center's raised, embossed seal. You must retain the original AKTR.

An AKTR with passing results is valid for 24 calendar months. To exercise the privileges of the Remote Pilot Certificate with a Small UAS Rating, you must comply with 14 CFR §107.65.

To obtain a duplicate AKTR due to loss or destruction of the original, mail a signed request accompanied by a check or money order made payable to the FAA in the amount of $12.00 the following address:

Federal Aviation Administration
Airmen Certification Branch, AFS-760
P.O. Box 25082
Oklahoma City, OK 73125

To obtain a copy of the application form or a list of the information required, please see the AFS-760 web page.

Test Tips

When taking a knowledge test, please keep the following points in mind:

1. Carefully read the instructions provided with the test.

2. Answer each question in accordance with the latest regulations and guidance publications.

3. Read each question carefully before looking at the answer options. You should clearly understand the problem before trying to solve it.

4. After formulating a response, determine which answer option corresponds with your answer. The answer you choose should completely solve the problem.

5. Remember that only one answer is complete and correct. The other possible answers are either incomplete or erroneous.

6. If a certain question is difficult for you, mark it for review and return to it after you have answered the less difficult questions. This procedure will enable you to use the available time to maximum advantage.

7. When solving a calculation problem, be sure to read all the associated notes.

8. For questions involving use of a graph, you may request a printed copy that you can mark in computing your answer. This copy and all other notes and paperwork must be given to the testing center upon completion of the test.

Eligibility Requirements for the Remote Pilot Certificate

When applying for a Remote Pilot Certificate with a Small UAS Rating, in addition to the eligibility requirements of 14 CFR §107.61, you must meet one of the following:

- Applicant must provide an Airman Knowledge Test Report (AKTR), which shows that you have passed the UAG aeronautical knowledge test as described in §107.73.

- If you hold a pilot certificate issued under Part 61 and meet the recency requirements specified in §61.56, you must provide a certificate of completion of a Part 107 initial training course. A qualifying initial training course is available at **www.faasafety.gov**. You must also show, via logbook entry or other method acceptable to the Administrator, that you meet the flight review requirements of §61.56.

The application must be submitted to a Flight Standards District Office (FSDO), a designated pilot examiner (DPE), an airman certification representative for a pilot school, a certified flight instructor (CFI), or other person authorized by the Administrator to process the application.

English Language Proficiency

In accordance with the requirements of 14 CFR §107.61(b) and the FAA Aviation English Language Proficiency standard, throughout the application and testing process, you must demonstrate the ability to read, write, speak, and understand the English language.

Knowledge Exam References

The FAA references the following documents to write the FAA Knowledge Exam questions. You should be familiar with all of these as part of your ground school studies, which you should complete before starting test preparation:

14 CFR Part 48 Registration and Marking Requirements for Unmanned Aircraft Systems
14 CFR Part 71 Designation of Class A, B, C, D and E Airspace Areas; Air Traffic Service Routes; and Reporting Points
14 CFR Part 107 Operation and Certification of Small Unmanned Aircraft Systems

FAA-H-8083-2 *Risk Management Handbook*
FAA-H-8083-25 *Pilot's Handbook of Aeronautical Knowledge*
FAA-H-8083-3 *Airplane Flying Handbook*
FAA-G-8082-22 *Remote Pilot sUAS Study Guide*

AC 00-6 *Aviation Weather*
AC 00-45 *Aviation Weather Services*
AC 60-22 *Aeronautical Decision Making*
AC 91-57 *Model Aircraft Operating Standards*
AC 150-5200-32 *Reporting Wildlife Aircraft Strikes*
AC 107-2 *Small Unmanned Aircraft Systems (sUAS)*

Aeronautical Information Manual (AIM)

Chart Supplement U.S. (formerly *Airport/Facility Directory* or A/FD)

SAFO 09013 *Fighting Fires Caused By Lithium Type Batteries in Portable Electronic Devices*
SAFO 10015 *Flying in the Wire Environment*
SAFO 10017 *Risks in Transporting Lithium Batteries in Cargo by Aircraft*
SAFO 15010 *Carriage of Spare Lithium Batteries in Carry-on and Checked Baggage*

Visit the ASA website for these and many more titles and pilot supplies for your aviation endeavors: **www.asa2fly.com**

Visit the Reader Resource for this book (**www.asa2fly.com/reader/TPUAS**) for additional resources useful to both remote pilots and manned pilots operating in the presence of unmanned aircraft systems.

ASA Test Prep Layout

The sample FAA questions have been sorted into chapters according to subject matter. Within each chapter, the questions have been further classified and all similar questions grouped together with a concise discussion of the material covered in each group. This discussion material of "Chapter text" is printed in a larger font and spans the entire width of the page. Immediately following the sample FAA Question is ASA's Explanation in *italics*. The last line of the Explanation contains the Learning Statement Code and further reference (if applicable). *See* the EXAMPLE below.

Figures referenced by the Chapter text only are numbered with the appropriate chapter number, i.e., "Figure 1-1" is Chapter 1's first chapter-text figure.

Some Questions refer to Figures or Legends immediately following the question number, i.e., "1201. (Refer to Figure 2.)." These are FAA Figures and Legends which can be found in the FAA *Airman Knowledge Testing Supplement* (CT-8080-2G). This supplement is bundled with the Test Prep and is the exact material you will have access to when you take your computerized test. We provide it separately, so you will become accustomed to referring to the FAA Figures and Legends as you would during the test.

Answers to each question are found at the bottom of each page.

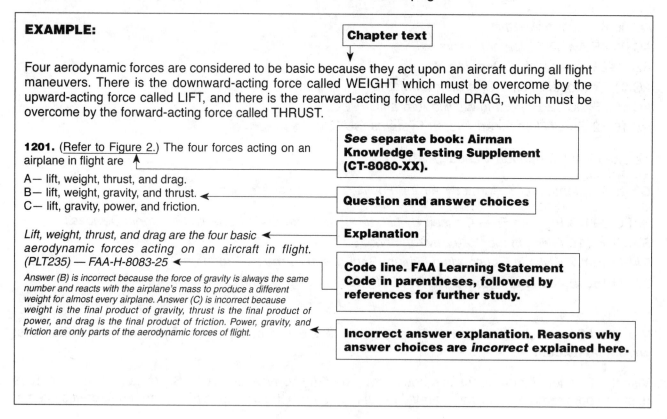

EXAMPLE:

Chapter text

Four aerodynamic forces are considered to be basic because they act upon an aircraft during all flight maneuvers. There is the downward-acting force called WEIGHT which must be overcome by the upward-acting force called LIFT, and there is the rearward-acting force called DRAG, which must be overcome by the forward-acting force called THRUST.

1201. (Refer to Figure 2.) The four forces acting on an airplane in flight are

A— lift, weight, thrust, and drag.
B— lift, weight, gravity, and thrust.
C— lift, gravity, power, and friction.

Lift, weight, thrust, and drag are the four basic aerodynamic forces acting on an aircraft in flight. (PLT235) — FAA-H-8083-25

Answer (B) is incorrect because the force of gravity is always the same number and reacts with the airplane's mass to produce a different weight for almost every airplane. Answer (C) is incorrect because weight is the final product of gravity, thrust is the final product of power, and drag is the final product of friction. Power, gravity, and friction are only parts of the aerodynamic forces of flight.

See separate book: Airman Knowledge Testing Supplement (CT-8080-XX).

Question and answer choices

Explanation

Code line. FAA Learning Statement Code in parentheses, followed by references for further study.

Incorrect answer explanation. Reasons why answer choices are *incorrect* explained here.

Chapter 1
Regulations

Introduction

The Federal Aviation Administration (FAA) has adopted specific rules to allow the operation of civil **small unmanned aircraft systems (sUAS)** in the **National Airspace System (NAS)** for purposes other than hobby and recreation. The rules are specified in Title 14 of the Code of Federal Regulations (14 CFR) Part 107, "Small Unmanned Aircraft Systems." Part 107 addresses sUAS classification, certification, and operational limitations and applies to the operation of certain civil small unmanned aircraft within the NAS. Except for certain excluded aircraft operations, any aircraft that meets the criteria below is considered a small unmanned aircraft.

Small unmanned aircraft:

- Weigh less than 55 pounds (25 kg), including everything that is onboard or otherwise attached to the aircraft.

- Are operated without the possibility of direct human intervention from within or on the aircraft.

You will see a number of different terms throughout this book used to refer to sUAS. This includes unmanned aircraft, small unmanned aircraft, UA, UAS, and sUAS. Any of these terms may be found on your FAA Knowledge Exam.

An sUAS includes the unmanned aircraft itself and its associated elements that are required for safe operation, such as communication links and components that control the aircraft.

Not all small unmanned aircraft are subject to 14 CFR Part 107. Part 107 does not apply to model aircraft that meet the criteria in 14 CFR §101.41 (for aircraft that meet the conditions in section 336 of Public Law 112-95), e.g. amateur rockets, moored balloons or unmanned free balloons, kites, operations conducted outside the United States, public aircraft operations, and air carrier operations. Hobbyists conducting recreational operations should follow the procedures in Advisory Circular (AC) 91-57, *Model Aircraft Operating Standards*, as well as 14 CFR §§101.41 and 101.43.

An in-flight emergency is an unexpected and unforeseen serious occurrence or situation that requires urgent, prompt action. In case of an in-flight emergency, the remote pilot-in-command (PIC) is permitted to deviate from any rule of Part 107 to the extent necessary to respond to that emergency. A remote PIC who exercises this emergency power to deviate from the rules of Part 107 is required, upon FAA request, to send a written report to the FAA explaining the deviation. Emergency action should be taken in such a way as to minimize injury or damage to property.

The following defined terms are pertinent to the Remote Pilot with an sUAS rating:

control station (CS)—An interface used by the remote pilot or the person manipulating the controls to control the flight path of the small UA.

corrective lenses—Spectacles or contact lenses.

model aircraft—A UA that is:

- Capable of sustained flight in the atmosphere;

- Flown within **visual line-of-sight (VLOS)** of the person operating the aircraft; and

- Flown for hobby or recreational purposes.

person manipulating the controls—A person other than the remote pilot-in-command (PIC) who is controlling the flight of an sUAS under the supervision of the remote PIC.

public aircraft—Means any of the following:

- An aircraft used only for the United States Government.

- An aircraft owned by the United States government and operated by any person for purposes related to crew training, equipment development, or demonstration.

Continued

- An aircraft owned and operated by the government of a State, the District of Columbia, or a territory or possession of the United States or a political subdivision of one of these governments.

- An aircraft exclusively leased for at least 90 continuous days by the government of a state, the District of Columbia, or a territory or possession of the United States or a political subdivision of one of these governments.

- An aircraft owned or operated by the armed forces or chartered to provide transportation or other commercial air service to the armed forces.

remote pilot-in-command (remote PIC or remote pilot)—A person who holds a remote pilot certificate with an sUAS rating and has the final authority and responsibility for the operation and safety of an sUAS operation conducted under Part 107.

small unmanned aircraft (UA)—A UA weighing less than 55 pounds, including everything that is onboard or otherwise attached to the aircraft, and can be flown without the possibility of direct human intervention from within or on the aircraft.

small unmanned aircraft system (sUAS)—A small UA and its associated elements (including communication links and the components that control the small UA) that are required for the safe and efficient operation of the small UA in the NAS.

unmanned aircraft (UA)—An aircraft operated without the possibility of direct human intervention from within or on the aircraft.

visual observer (VO)—A person acting as a flightcrew member who assists the small UA remote PIC and the person manipulating the controls to see and avoid other air traffic or objects aloft or on the ground.

1001. You are operating a 1,280 g (2.8 lb) quadcopter for your own enjoyment. What FAA regulation is this sUAS operation subject to?

A— 14 CFR Part 107.
B— 14 CFR Part 48.
C— This operation is not subject to FAA regulations.

This operation is recreational in nature. However, Part 48 "Registration and Marking Requirements for sUAS" applies for all operations of an sUAS over .55 pounds, whether for work or your own enjoyment. (PLT443) — 14 CFR §107.3

1002. You have accepted football tickets in exchange for using your sUAS to videotape a future construction zone. What FAA regulation is this sUAS operation subject to?

A— 14 CFR Part 107.
B— 14 CFR Part 101.
C— This operation is not subject to FAA regulations.

This sUAS operation is subject to 14 CFR Part 107 because compensation (money or otherwise) makes the operation commercial in nature. (PLT448) — 14 CFR §107.3

1003. You plan to operate a 33 lb sUAS to capture aerial imagery over real estate for use in sales listings. What FAA regulation is this sUAS operation subject to?

A— 14 CFR Part 107.
B— 14 CFR Part 101.
C— This operation is not subject to FAA regulations.

This sUAS operation is subject to 14 CFR Part 107 because the aerial imagery is for the furtherance of a business, making it commercial in nature. (PLT448) — 14 CFR §107.3

1004. According to 14 CFR Part 107, an sUAS is an unmanned aircraft system weighing

A— less than 55 lbs.
B— 55 kg or less.
C— 55 lbs or less.

Small unmanned aircraft (sUAS) means an unmanned aircraft weighing less than 55 pounds on takeoff, including everything that is on board or otherwise attached to the aircraft. (PLT395) — 14 CFR §107.1, AC 107-2

Answers

1001 [B]   1002 [A]   1003 [A]   1004 [A]

1005. "Unmanned aircraft" is defined as a device operated

A— during search and rescue operations other than public.
B— without the possibility of direct human intervention from within or on the aircraft.
C— for hobby and recreational use when not certificated.

An unmanned aircraft means an aircraft operated without the possibility of direct human intervention from within or on the aircraft. (PLT395) — 14 CFR §§107.1 and 107.3, AC 107-2

1006. Which of the following types of operations are excluded from the requirements in 14 CFR Part 107?

A— Model aircraft for hobby use.
B— Quadcopter capturing aerial imagery for crop monitoring.
C— UAS used for motion picture filming.

14 CFR Part 107 does not apply to model aircraft that meet the criteria in 14 CFR §101.41, amateur rockets, moored balloons or unmanned free balloons, kites, operations conducted outside the United States, public aircraft operations, and air carrier operations. (PLT448) — 14 CFR §107.1, AC 107-2

1007. Which of the following operations would be regulated by 14 CFR Part 107?

A— Conducting public operations during a search mission.
B— Flying for enjoyment with family and friends.
C— Operating your sUAS for an imagery company.

Part 107 regulates commercial sUAS operations. (PLT448) — 14 CFR §§107.41 and 107.1

1008. As a remote pilot with an sUAS rating, under which situation can you deviate from 14 CFR Part 107?

A— When conducting public operations during a search mission.
B— Flying for enjoyment with family and friends.
C— In response to an in-flight emergency.

In case of an in-flight emergency, the remote PIC is permitted to deviate from any rule of Part 107 to the extent necessary to respond to that emergency. (PLT444) — 14 CFR §107.21

1009. What action, if any, is appropriate if the remote pilot deviates from Part 107 during an emergency?

A— Take no special action since you are pilot-in-command.
B— File a detailed report to the FAA Administrator, upon request.
C— File a report to the FAA Administrator, as soon as possible.

Each remote PIC who deviates from a rule in Part 107 must, upon request of the FAA Administrator, send a written report of that deviation to the Administrator. (PLT403) — 14 CFR §107.21

1280. Which of these operations must comply with 14 CFR Part 107?

A— Civil operations.
B— Civil and public operations.
C— Public and military operations.

Part 107 addresses sUAS operations of certain civil small unmanned aircraft within the National Airspace System. (PLT528) — 14 CFR Part 107

1010. To avoid a possible collision with a manned airplane, you estimate that your small unmanned aircraft climbed to an altitude greater than 600 feet AGL. To whom must you report the deviation?

A— Upon request of the Federal Aviation Administration.
B— The National Transportation Safety Board.
C— Air Traffic Control.

Each remote PIC who deviates from a rule in Part 107 must, upon request of the FAA Administrator, send a written report of that deviation to the Administrator. (PLT403) — 14 CFR §107.21

1011. When an ATC clearance has been obtained, no remote PIC may deviate from that clearance, unless that pilot obtains an amended clearance. The one exception to this regulation is

A— when the clearance states "at pilot's discretion."
B— an emergency.
C— if the clearance contains a restriction.

Except in an emergency, no person may operate an aircraft contrary to an ATC clearance or instruction. (PLT403) — 14 CFR §107.21

Answers

1005 [B]	1006 [A]	1007 [C]	1008 [C]	1009 [B]	1280 [A]
1010 [A]	1011 [B]				

Remote Pilot Certification

When a pilot certificate is issued, it lists the certification level which defines the privileges and limitations of that certificate holder, such as Remote Pilot, Private Pilot, Flight Instructor, or Airline Transport Pilot (ATP). Additionally, the issued pilot certificate will include the category of aircraft in which the certificate holder is qualified. The term "category" means a broad classification of aircraft, such as airplane, rotorcraft, glider, and lighter-than-air. Small unmanned aircraft (sUAS) is a "rating."

An sUAS operation may involve one individual or a team of crewmembers. These sUAS crew roles include:

- Remote PIC—a person who holds a current remote pilot certificate with an sUAS rating and has the final authority and responsibility for the operation and safety of the sUAS.

- Person manipulating the controls—a person controlling the sUAS under direct supervision of the remote PIC, or the remote PIC themselves, if controlling the sUAS.

- Visual observer (VO)—a person acting as a flight crewmember to help see and avoid air traffic or other objects in the sky, overhead, or on the ground.

In the aviation context, the FAA typically refers to "licensing" as "certification." Just like a manned aircraft pilot-in-command, the remote PIC of an sUAS is directly responsible for, and is the final authority as to the operation of that UAS. The remote PIC will have final authority over the flight. Additionally, a person manipulating the controls can participate in flight operations under certain conditions.

A person acting as a remote PIC of an sUAS in the National Airspace System under Part 107 must obtain a Remote Pilot certificate with an sUAS rating issued by the FAA prior to sUAS operation. The remote PIC must have this certificate easily accessible during flight operations.

To apply for a Part 107 remote pilot certificate with an sUAS rating, you must satisfy the following eligibility requirements:

- Be at least 16 years old

- Be able to read, speak, write, and understand the English language (FAA may make exceptions for medical reasons)

- Be in a physical and mental condition that would not interfere with the safe operation of sUAS

- Fulfill training and testing requirements (defined in 14 CFR Part 107)

Applicants for a Part 107 Remote Pilot certificate with an sUAS rating must meet the following requirements in order to gain and retain the knowledge necessary to safely operate UAS in the NAS.

Applicant	Initial Requirements	Recurrent Requirements (every 24 months)
Part 61 Pilot Certificate Holder with a Current Flight Review (per 14 CFR Part §61.56)	The **faasafety.gov** initial online course, or the FAA UAG Knowledge Exam	The recurrent online course, or the FAA UAG Knowledge Exam
Any Other Applicant	The FAA UAG Knowledge Exam	The FAA UAG Knowledge Exam

After you satisfy the applicable training or testing requirements, you may apply for a Part 107 Remote Pilot certificate with an sUAS rating through an online or paper process. The FAA encourages the use of an online application through the **Integrated Airman Certificate and/or Rating Application (IACRA)**. A paper process is available using FAA Form 8710-13, *Remote Pilot Certificate and/or Rating Application*, however the paper application requires increased processing time and will delay the issuance of your permanent certificate. The application must be submitted to a **Flight Standards District**

Office (FSDO), a designated pilot examiner (DPE), an airman certification representative for a pilot school, a certified flight instructor (CFI), or other person authorized by an FAA Administrator to process the application. A temporary certificate will be issued, valid until receipt of the permanent certificate or for up to 120 calendar days.

After the FAA receives the application, the Transportation Security Administration (TSA) will automatically conduct a background security screening of the applicant prior to issuance of a remote pilot certificate. If the security screening is successful, the FAA will issue a permanent remote pilot certificate. If the security screening is not successful, the applicant will be disqualified and a pilot certificate will not be issued. Individuals who believe that they improperly failed a security threat assessment may appeal the decision to the TSA.

Remote Pilot certificate holders with an sUAS rating must meet the recurrent training requirements every 24 months. This retraining can be satisfied by completing the online FAA course or taking the FAA Knowledge Exam.

1012. Which of the following individuals may process an application for a Part 107 Remote Pilot certificate with an sUAS rating?

A— Commercial balloon pilot.
B— Remote pilot in command.
C— Designated Pilot Examiner.

The remote pilot application must be submitted to a Flight Standards District Office (FSDO), a designated pilot examiner (DPE), an airman certification representative for a pilot school, a certified flight instructor (CFI), or other person authorized by the Administrator to process the application. (PLT448) — 14 CFR §§107.63 and 61.56

1013. After receiving a Part 107 remote pilot certificate with an sUAS rating, how often must you satisfy recurrent training requirements?

A— Every 6 months.
B— Every 12 months.
C— Every 24 months.

Remote Pilot certificate holders with an sUAS rating must meet the recurrent training requirements every 24 months. This retraining can be satisfied by completing the online FAA course or taking the FAA Knowledge Exam. (PLT442) — 14 CFR Part §§107.63 and 107.65, AC 107-2

1014. To satisfy medical requirements, all sUAS crewmembers must

A— hold a valid third-class medical certificate.
B— be free of any physical or mental condition that would interfere with the safe operation of the small unmanned aircraft system.
C— complete a physical with an Aviation Medical Examiner.

No person may manipulate the flight controls of a small unmanned aircraft system or act as a remote pilot-in-command, visual observer, or direct participant in the operation of the small unmanned aircraft if he or she knows or has reason to know that he or she has a physical or mental condition that would interfere with the safe operation of the small unmanned aircraft system. (PLT427) — 14 CFR §107.17

1015. Which of the following would medically disqualify a Remote Pilot?

A— Taking a prescription medication that does not have any noticeable side effects.
B— A migraine headache with the side effect of blurred vision.
C— Occasional muscle soreness following exercise.

No person may manipulate the flight controls of an sUAS or act as a remote PIC, visual observer, or direct participant in the operation of the small unmanned aircraft if he or she knows or has reason to know that he or she has a physical or mental condition that would interfere with the safe operation of the sUAS. (PLT427) — 14 CFR §107.17

Answers
1012 [C]   1013 [C]   1014 [B]   1015 [B]

Remote Pilot Privileges

The remote PIC is directly responsible for and is the final authority as to the operation of the sUAS conducted under 14 CFR Part 107. He or she must:

- Be designated before each flight (but can change during the flight).
- Ensure that the operation poses no undue hazard to people, aircraft, or property in the event of a loss of control of the aircraft for any reason.
- Operate the small unmanned aircraft to ensure compliance with all applicable provisions and regulations.

Being able to safely operate the sUAS relies on, among other things, the physical and mental capabilities of the remote PIC, person manipulating the controls, VO, and any other direct participant in the sUAS operation. Though the person manipulating the controls of an sUAS and VO are not required to obtain an airman medical certificate, they may not participate in the operation of an sUAS if they know or have reason to know that they have a physical or mental condition that could interfere with the safe operation of the sUAS.

A person may not operate or act as a remote PIC or VO in the operation of more than one UA at the same time. Additionally, Part 107 allows transfer of control of an sUAS between certificated remote pilots. Two or more certificated remote pilots transferring operational control (i.e., the remote PIC designation) to each other may do so only if they are both capable of maintaining VLOS of the UA and without loss of control (LOC). For example, one remote pilot may be designated the remote PIC at the beginning of the operation, and then at some point in the operation another remote pilot may take over as remote PIC by positively communicating that he or she is doing so. As the person responsible for the safe operation of the UAS, any remote pilot who will assume remote PIC duties should meet all of the requirements of Part 107, including awareness of factors that could affect the flight.

1016. Who is responsible for ensuring that there are enough crewmembers for a given sUAS operation?

A— Remote pilot in command.
B— Person manipulating the controls.
C— Visual observer.

The remote PIC is ultimately responsible for assessing the needs of the operation and preparing sufficient support crewmembers to ensure the safety of the operation. (PLT440) — 14 CFR §107.12

1017. Who is ultimately responsible for preventing a hazardous situation before an accident occurs?

A— Remote pilot in command.
B— Person manipulating the controls.
C— Visual observer.

The remote PIC is ultimately responsible for identifying hazards and taking appropriate action (or intervening when another person is manipulating the controls) to ensure the safety of the flight. (PLT440) — 14 CFR §107.12

1018. Which crewmember must hold a remote pilot certificate with an sUAS rating?

A— Remote pilot in command.
B— Person manipulating the controls.
C— Visual observer.

The remote PIC must hold a Part 107 remote pilot certificate with an sUAS rating before conducting any sUAS operation. (PLT443) — 14 CFR §107.12

1019. When using a small unmanned aircraft in a commercial operation, who is responsible for briefing the participants about emergency procedures?

A— The lead visual observer.
B— The FAA inspector-in-charge.
C— The remote pilot in command.

Prior to flight, the remote PIC must ensure that all persons directly participating in the small unmanned aircraft operation are informed about the operating conditions, emergency procedures, contingency procedures, roles and responsibilities, and potential hazards. (PLT441) — 14 CFR §107.49, AC 107-2

Answers

1016 [A]   1017 [A]   1018 [A]   1019 [C]

1020. The remote PIC may operate how many sUAS at a time?

A— 1.
B— 5.
C— No more than 2.

A person may not operate or act as a remote pilot-in-command or visual observer in the operation of more than one unmanned aircraft at the same time. (PLT373) — 14 CFR §107.35

Supporting Crew Roles

A person who does not hold a remote pilot certificate or a remote pilot that that has not met the recurrent testing/training requirements of Part 107 may operate the flight controls of an sUAS under Part 107, as long as he or she is directly supervised by a remote PIC and the remote PIC has the ability to immediately take direct control of the sUAS. This ability is necessary to ensure that the remote PIC can quickly address any hazardous situation before an accident occurs.

The remote PIC can take over the flight controls by using a number of different methods. For example, the operation could involve a "buddy box" type of system that uses two **control stations (CS)**: one for the person manipulating the flight controls, and one for the remote PIC that allows the remote PIC to override the other CS and immediately take direct control of the small UA. Another method involves the remote PIC standing close enough to the person manipulating the flight controls to be able to physically take over the CS from that person. A third method could employ the use of an automation system whereby the remote PIC could immediately engage that system to put the small UA in a pre-programmed "safe" mode (such as in a hover, in a holding pattern, or "return home").

An **autonomous operation** is when the autopilot onboard the UA performs certain functions without direct pilot input. For example, the remote pilot can input a flight route into the CS, which then sends it to the autopilot that is installed in the small UA. During autonomous flight, flight control inputs are made by components onboard the aircraft, not from a CS. Thus, the remote PIC could lose the control link to the small UA and the aircraft would still continue to fly the programmed mission and/or return home to land.

When the UA is flying autonomously, the remote PIC also must have the ability to change routing or altitude, or to command the aircraft to land immediately. The ability to direct the small UA may be through manual manipulation of the flight controls or through commands using automation. The remote PIC must retain the ability to direct the small UA to ensure compliance with the requirements of Part 107. There are different methods a remote PIC may utilize to direct the small UA to ensure compliance with Part 107. For example, the remote PIC may transmit a command for the autonomous aircraft to climb, descend, land now, proceed to a new waypoint, enter an orbit pattern, or return to home. Any of these methods may be used to satisfactorily avoid a hazard or give right-of-way. The use of automation does not allow a person to simultaneously operate more than one small UA.

The role of visual observers (VOs) is to alert the rest of the crew about potential hazards during sUAS operations. The use of VOs is optional. However, the remote PIC may use one or more VOs to supplement situational awareness and VLOS responsibilities while the remote PIC is conducting other mission-critical duties (such as checking displays). The remote PIC must make certain that all VOs:

• Are positioned in a location where they are able to see the sUAS continuously and sufficiently to maintain VLOS.

• Possess a means to effectively communicate the sUAS position and the position of other aircraft to the remote PIC and person manipulating the controls.

Continued

Answers

1020 [A]

1021. Which crewmember is required to be under the direct supervision of the remote PIC when operating an sUAS?

A— Remote pilot in command.
B— Person manipulating the controls.
C— Visual observer.

A non-certificated person may manipulate the controls of the sUAS only if he or she is under the direct supervision of the remote PIC. (PLT373) — 14 CFR §107.12

1022. A person without a Part 107 Remote Pilot certificate may operate an sUAS for commercial operations

A— under the direct supervision of a remote PIC.
B— only when visual observers participate in the operation.
C— alone, if operating during daylight hours.

A person who does not hold a Remote Pilot certificate or a remote pilot that that has not met the recurrent testing/training requirements of Part 107 may operate the sUAS under Part 107, as long as he or she is directly supervised by a remote PIC and the remote PIC has the ability to immediately take direct control of the sUAS. (PLT373) — 14 CFR §107.12

1023. Whose sole task during an sUAS operation is to watch the sUAS and report potential hazards to the rest of the crew?

A— Remote pilot in command.
B— Person manipulating the controls.
C— Visual observer.

The visual observer (when asked by the remote PIC) maintains visual line of sight with the sUAS and reports any potential hazards to the remote PIC and person manipulating the controls. (PLT440) — 14 CFR §107.33

1024. Which of the following crewmembers must be used during Part 107 sUAS operations?

A— Remote PIC.
B— Remote PIC and visual observer.
C— Remote PIC, visual observer, and person manipulating the controls.

A remote pilot-in-command must be used during Part 107 sUAS operations. A visual observer is optional. The person manipulating the controls may be the remote PIC, or must be operating under the direct supervision of the remote PIC. (PLT440) — 14 CFR §107.19

1025. An autonomous operation requires the following crewmembers.

A— Remote PIC.
B— Remote PIC and visual observer.
C— Remote PIC, visual observer, and person manipulating the controls.

An autonomous operation does not negate the requirement for a remote PIC. An autonomous operation is generally considered an operation in which the remote pilot inputs a flight plan into the control station, which sends it to the autopilot onboard the small UA. (PLT440) — AC 107-2

Falsification, Reproduction, or Alteration

The FAA relies on information provided by owners and remote pilots of sUAS when it authorizes operations or when it has to make a compliance determination. Accordingly, the FAA may take appropriate action against an sUAS owner, operator, remote PIC, or anyone else who fraudulently or knowingly provides false records or reports, or otherwise reproduces or alters any records, reports, or other information for fraudulent purposes. Such action could include civil sanctions and the suspension or revocation of a certificate or waiver.

Answers

| 1021 [B] | 1022 [A] | 1023 [C] | 1024 [A] | 1025 [A] |

1026. Under Title 14 of the Code of Federal Regulations, what is the maximum penalty for falsification, alteration, or fraudulent reproduction of certificates, logbooks, reports, and records?

A— Ineligibility to receive any certificate or rating for one year.

B— Imprisonment for one year and a $5,000.00 fine.

C— Suspension or revocation of any certificate held.

14 CFR §65.20 states that any person who falsifies or makes a fraudulent entry in a logbook, report, or record is subject to the suspension or revocation of any airman or ground instructor certificate or rating held by that person. (PLT454) — 14 CFR §107.5

Accident Reporting

The remote PIC must report any sUAS accident to the FAA, within 10 days of the operation, if any of the following thresholds are met:

- Serious injury to any person or any loss of consciousness.
- Damage to any property, other than the small unmanned aircraft, if the cost is greater than $500 to repair or replace the property (whichever is lower).

For example, a small UA damages property of which the fair market value is $200, and it would cost $600 to repair the damage. Because the fair market value is below $500, this accident is not required to be reported. Similarly, if the aircraft causes $200 worth of damage to property whose fair market value is $600, that accident is also not required to be reported because the repair cost is below $500.

The accident report must be made within 10 calendar-days of the operation that created the injury or damage. The report may be submitted to the appropriate **FAA Regional Operations Center (ROC)** or FSDO electronically (**www.faa.gov/uas**) or by telephone. The report should include the following information:

1. sUAS remote PIC's name and contact information;
2. sUAS remote PIC's FAA airman certificate number;
3. sUAS registration number issued to the aircraft, if required (FAA registration number);
4. Location of the accident;
5. Date of the accident;
6. Time of the accident;
7. Person(s) injured and extent of injury, if any or known;
8. Property damaged and extent of damage, if any or known; and
9. Description of what happened.

A serious injury qualifies as Level 3 or higher on the **Abbreviated Injury Scale (AIS)** of the Association for the Advancement of Automotive Medicine. This scale is an anatomical scoring system that is widely used by emergency medical personnel. In the AIS system, injuries are ranked on a scale of 1 to 6; Level 1 is a minor injury, Level 2 is moderate, Level 3 is serious, Level 4 is severe, Level 5 is critical, and Level 6 is a nonsurvivable injury. It would be considered a serious injury if a person requires hospitalization, and the injury is fully reversible including, but not limited to:

Continued

Answers

1026 [C]

- Head trauma.
- Broken bone(s).
- Laceration(s) to the skin that requires suturing.

In addition to this FAA report, and in accordance with the criteria established by the National Transportation Safety Board (NTSB), certain sUAS accidents must also be reported to the NTSB.

1027. You are part of a news crew, operating an sUAS to cover a breaking story. You experience a flyaway during landing. The unmanned aircraft strikes a vehicle, causing approximately $800 worth of damage. When must you report the accident to the FAA?

A— Anytime.
B— Within 10 days.
C— Not to exceed 30 days.

Report any sUAS accident to the FAA within 10 days if it results in serious injury, loss of consciousness, or repairs costing over $500. (PLT366) — 14 CFR §107.9

1028. Within how many days must an sUAS accident be reported to the FAA?

A— 90 days.
B— 10 days.
C— 30 days.

Report any sUAS accident to the FAA within 10 days if it results in serious injury, loss of consciousness, or repairs costing over $500. (PLT366) — 14 CFR §107.9

1029. While operating a small unmanned aircraft system (sUAS), you experience a flyaway and several people suffer injuries. Which of the following injuries requires reporting to the FAA?

A— An injury requiring an overnight hospital stay.
B— Scrapes and cuts bandaged on site.
C— Minor bruises.

The remote PIC must report any sUAS accident to the FAA, within 10 days of the operation, if a serious injury to any person or any loss of consciousness occurs. It would be considered a serious injury if a person requires hospitalization. (PLT366) — 14 CFR §107.9, AC 107-2

1030. As you are flying your sUAS, valued at $1,000, over a home to photograph it for real estate sales purposes, the sUAS has a failure causing it to fall onto an awning causing some minor damage. The fair market value of the awning is $800 but it can be repaired for $400. What type of report is required?

A— An sUAS accident report to the FAA, within 10 days of the operation.
B— An sUAS incident report to the FAA, within 10 days of the operation.
C— No report is required.

No report is required because the damage can be repaired for less than $500. A report is required only when damage to any property, other than the small UA, is greater than $500 to repair or replace the property (whichever is lower). The cost of the sUAS is not considered when determining if an event is considered to be an accident or incident. (PLT366) — 14 CFR §107.9, AC 107-2

Answers

1027 [B]   1028 [B]   1029 [A]   1030 [C]

FAA Inspections

You must make available to the FAA, upon request, the sUAS for inspection or testing. In addition, you must verify before flight that all required documentation is physically or electronically available in the event of an on-site FAA inspection. Such documentation may include:

- Pilot certificate;
- Aircraft registration;
- Any necessary waiver or exemption; or
- Other documentation related to the operation.

1031. When must a current remote pilot certificate be in the pilot's personal possession or readily accessible in the aircraft?

A— When acting as a crew chief during launch and recovery.

B— Only when a payload is carried.

C— Anytime when acting as pilot-in-command or as a required crewmember.

No person may act as pilot-in-command (PIC), or in any other capacity as a required pilot flight crewmember when operating a sUAS unless he or she has in possession or readily accessible a current pilot certificate. (PLT448) — 14 CFR §107.7

1032. Each person who holds a pilot certificate, a U.S. driver's license, or a medical certificate shall present it for inspection upon the request of the Administrator, the National Transportation Safety Board, or any

A— authorized representative of the Administrator of the Department of Transportation.

B— authorized representative of the Department of State.

C— federal, state, or local law enforcement officer.

A remote pilot-in-command, owner, or person manipulating the flight controls of a small unmanned aircraft system must, upon request, make available to the Administrator: (1) the remote pilot certificate with a small UAS rating; and (2) any other document, record, or report required. (PLT448) — 14 CFR §107.7

1304. If requested, to whom must I present my Remote Pilot Certificate?

A— A person of authority.

B— FAA Inspector.

C— Authorized representative of the Department of State.

A remote pilot-in-command, owner, or person manipulating the flight controls of a small unmanned aircraft system must, upon request, make available to the Administrator: (1) the remote pilot certificate with a small UAS rating; and (2) any other document, record, or report required. (PLT442) — 14 CFR §107.7

sUAS Registration

Most sUAS must be registered with the FAA prior to operating in the NAS. Owners must register the sUAS if it is greater than 0.55 pounds, less than 55 pounds, and operated under the provisions of 14 CFR Part 107. The owner must satisfy the registration requirements described in 14 CFR Part 47, "Aircraft Registration," or Part 48, "Registration and Marking Requirements for Small Unmanned Aircraft." The sUAS must be registered by a person who is at least 13 years of age. 14 CFR Part 48 establishes the online registration option for sUAS that will be operated only within the territorial limits of the United States.

An sUAS operation requires a Foreign Aircraft Permit if it involves a civil aircraft that is:

- Registered in a foreign country; or
- Owned, controlled, or operated by someone who is not a U.S. citizen or permanent resident.

Continued

Answers

1031 [C]   1032 [A]   1304 [B]

If either criteria is met, the remote PIC should obtain a Foreign Aircraft Permit pursuant to 14 CFR §375.41 before conducting any operations.

Before operation, mark the sUAS to identify that it is registered with the FAA. The registration marking must be:

- A unique identifier number. This is typically the FAA-issued registration number or the serial number, if authorized during registration.
- Legible and durable. Sample methods include engraving, permanent marker, or self-adhesive label.
- Visible or accessible. The number may be enclosed in a compartment only if you can access the compartment without tools.

An FAA airworthiness certification is not required for sUAS. However, the remote PIC must maintain and inspect the sUAS prior to each flight to ensure that it is in a condition for safe operation. For example, inspect the aircraft for equipment damage or malfunctions.

1033. According to 14 CFR Part 48, when would a small unmanned aircraft owner not be permitted to register it?

A— All persons must register their small unmanned aircraft.
B— If the owner does not have a valid United States driver's license.
C— The owner is less than 13 years of age.

The sUAS must be registered by a person who is at least 13 years of age. (PLT530) — 14 CFR §§107.13 and 91.203

1034. According to 14 CFR Part 48, when must a person register a small UA with the Federal Aviation Administration?

A— All civilian small UAs weighing greater than .55 pounds must be registered regardless of its intended use.
B— When the small UA is used for any purpose other than as a model aircraft.
C— Only when the operator will be paid for commercial services.

Owners must register the sUAS if it is greater than 0.55 pounds, less than 55 pounds, and operated under the provisions of 14 CFR Part 107 which regulate commercial sUAS operations. (PLT530) — 14 CFR §107.13

1035. Under what conditions would a small unmanned aircraft not have to be registered before it is operated in the United States?

A— When the aircraft weighs less than .55 pounds on takeoff, including everything that is on-board or attached to the aircraft.
B— When the aircraft has a takeoff weight that is more than .55 pounds but less than 55 pounds, not including fuel and necessary attachments.
C— All small unmanned aircraft need to be registered regardless of the weight of the aircraft before, during, or after the flight.

Owners must register the sUAS if it is greater than 0.55 lbs, less than 55 pounds and operated under the provisions of 14 CFR Part 107. (PLT530) — 14 CFR §107.13

Answer (B) is incorrect because the question is asking when registration is not required. Answer (C) is incorrect because sUAS must be registered if the device is between 0.55 and 55 pounds.

Preflight Action and Inspection

The remote PIC must complete a preflight familiarization, inspection, and other actions, such as crewmember briefings, prior to beginning flight operations. Before beginning any sUAS flight operation:

- Assess the operating environment including local weather conditions, local airspace, flight restrictions, the location of persons and property on the surface, and other ground hazards.

Answers

1033 [C]   1034 [A]   1035 [A]

- Inform any supporting crewmembers about the operation and their roles including operating conditions, emergency procedures, contingency procedures, roles and responsibilities of each person involved in the operation, as well as potential hazards.
- Inspect the sUAS to see that it is in a condition for safe operation, ensuring that all control links between the control station and the small unmanned aircraft are working properly, there is sufficient power to continue controlled flight operations to a normal landing, any object attached or carried by the sUAS is secure and does not adversely affect the flight characteristics or controllability of the aircraft, and the unique identifier is readily accessible and visible upon inspection of the sUAS.
- Maintain documents required in the event of an on-site FAA inspection, including the remote PIC's Remote Pilot certificate, aircraft registration (if required), and Certificate of Waiver (CoW) (if applicable).

1036. According to 14 CFR Part 107, the responsibility to inspect the small unmanned aircraft system (sUAS) to ensure it is in safe operating condition rests with the

A— owner of the sUAS.
B— visual observer.
C— remote pilot-in-command.

The remote PIC must complete a preflight familiarization, inspection, and other actions, such as crewmember briefings, prior to beginning flight operations. (PLT372) — 14 CFR §107.49

1037. Which preflight action is specifically required of the pilot prior to each flight?

A— Check the aircraft logbooks for appropriate entries.
B— Assess the operating environment including local weather conditions, local airspace and any flight restrictions, the location of persons and property on the surface, and other ground hazards.
C— Visually inspect the pilot certificates of all crew members.

Each remote pilot shall, before each flight, assess the operating environment including local weather conditions, local airspace and any flight restrictions, the location of persons and property on the surface, and other ground hazards.(PLT445) — 14 CFR §107.49

Carriage of Hazardous Material

A small unmanned aircraft may not carry hazardous material. Hazardous material means a substance or material that the Secretary of Transportation has determined is capable of posing an unreasonable risk to health, safety, and property when transported in commerce. The term includes hazardous substances, hazardous wastes, marine pollutants, elevated temperature materials, and materials that meet the defining criteria for hazard classes and divisions in 49 CFR Part 173.

Lithium batteries that are installed in an sUAS for power during the operation are not considered a hazardous material under Part 107. However, spare (uninstalled) lithium batteries would meet the definition of hazardous material and may not be carried on the sUAS.

1038. Under what circumstances may lithium batteries be carried during sUAS operations?

A— Lithium batteries are prohibited from sUAS operations.
B— Lithium batteries may be carried in a sealed storage container away from the sUAS fuel source.
C— Lithium batteries may be carried only when installed as the primary power for the operation.

Lithium batteries that are installed in an sUAS for power during the operation are not considered a hazardous material under Part 107. However, spare (uninstalled) lithium batteries would meet the definition of hazardous material and may not be carried on the sUAS. (PLT405) — AC 107-2

Answers
1036 [C]   1037 [B]   1038 [C]

Daylight Operations

14 CFR Part 107 prohibits operation of a small UAS at night, defined in 14 CFR Part 1 as the time between the end of evening civil twilight and the beginning of morning civil twilight, as published in the Federal Air Almanac and converted to local time. The Federal Air Almanac provides tables to determine sunrise and sunset at various latitudes. For example:

- In the contiguous United States, evening civil twilight is the period from sunset until 30 minutes after sunset and morning civil twilight is the period of 30 minutes prior to sunrise until sunrise.

- In Alaska, the definition of civil twilight differs and is described in the Federal Air Almanac.

When sUAS operations are conducted during civil twilight, the sUAS must be equipped with anti-collision lights that are capable of being visible for at least 3 statute miles. However, the remote PIC may reduce the intensity of the lighting if he or she has determined that it would be in the interest of operational safety to do so. For example, the remote PIC may momentarily reduce the lighting intensity if it impacts his or her night vision.

1039. According to 14 CFR Part 107, what is required to operate a small unmanned aircraft within 30 minutes after official sunset?

A— Use of a transponder.
B— Use of lighted anti-collision lights.
C— Must be operated in a rural area.

When sUAS operations are conducted during civil twilight, the sUAS must be equipped with anti-collision lights that are capable of being visible for at least 3 statute miles. (PLT119) — 14 CFR §107.29

1040. If sunset is 2021 and the end of evening civil twilight is 2043, when must a remote pilot terminate the flight?

A— 2021.
B— 2043.
C— 2121.

A remote pilot may not act as pilot-in-command of an sUAS at night. A remote pilot must land by the end of evening twilight. (PLT220) — 14 CFR §107.29

1274. Sunrise is 0645. When can you launch your sUAS operation?

A— 0645.
B— 0615.
C— 0715.

A remote pilot may not act as pilot-in-command of an sUAS at night. Night is defined as the time between the end of evening civil twilight and the beginning of morning civil twilight. Morning civil twilight is the period 30 minutes prior to sunrise until sunrise. This means you can launch your sUAS operation 30 minutes prior to sunrise. (PLT220) — 14 CFR §107.29

Visual Line of Sight

The sUAS must remain within VLOS of flight crewmembers. VLOS means any flight crewmember (i.e. the remote PIC, person manipulating the controls, and visual observers if used) is capable of seeing the aircraft with vision unaided by any device other than corrective lenses (spectacles or contact lenses). Vision aids, such as binoculars, may be used only momentarily to enhance situational awareness. For example, the remote PIC, person manipulating the controls, or visual observer may use vision aids briefly to avoid flying over persons or to avoid conflicting with other aircraft.

Crewmembers must be able to see the small unmanned aircraft at all times during flight. Therefore, the small unmanned aircraft must be operated closely enough to the CS to ensure visibility requirements are met during small unmanned aircraft operations. The VLOS requirement would not prohibit actions such as scanning the airspace or briefly looking down at the CS. The person maintaining VLOS may have

Answers

1039 [B]   1040 [B]   1274 [B]

brief moments in which he or she is not looking directly at or cannot see the small UA, but still retains the capability to see the UA or quickly maneuver it back to VLOS. These moments can be for the safety of the operation (e.g., looking at the controller to see battery life remaining) or for operational necessity.

For operational necessity, the remote PIC or person manipulating the controls may intentionally maneuver the UA so he or she loses sight of it for brief periods of time. Should the remote PIC or person manipulating the controls lose VLOS of the small UA, he or she must regain VLOS as soon as practicable. For example, a remote PIC stationed on the ground utilizing a small UA to inspect a rooftop may lose sight of the aircraft for brief periods while inspecting the farthest point of the roof. As another example, a remote PIC conducting a search operation around a fire scene with an sUAS may briefly lose sight of the aircraft while it is temporarily behind a dense column of smoke. Although this is a practical application, remote PICs must avoid interfering with emergency responders when operating in and around a fire scene.

Even though the remote PIC may briefly lose sight of the small UA, he or she always has the see-and-avoid responsibilities.

1041. Power company employees use an sUAS to inspect a long stretch of high voltage powerlines. Due to muddy conditions, their vehicle must stay beside the road and the crew must use binoculars to maintain visual line of sight with the aircraft. Is this sUAS operation in compliance with 14 CFR Part 107?

A— Yes, the operation is compliant with Part 107.
B— There is not enough information to make a determination.
C— No, the operation is not compliant with Part 107.

This scenario is not compliant with Part 107. Vision aids, such as binoculars may be used only momentarily to enhance situational awareness. They may not be used for the duration of the operation. (PLT373) — 14 CFR §107.31

1042. A crew conducting surveillance anticipates losing visual sight with the sUAS within a small segment of the flight plan. The flight

A— may be conducted using binoculars.
B— must be rerouted to maintain visual line of sight.
C— may be conducted if the visual line of sight can be maintained for 50% of the route.

The sUAS must remain within visual line-of-sight (VLOS) of flight crewmembers. The VLOS requirement would not prohibit actions such as scanning the airspace or briefly looking down at the sUAS control station. Should the remote PIC or person manipulating the controls lose VLOS of the small UA, he or she must regain VLOS as soon as possible. (PLT373) — 14 CFR §107.31

Answer (A) is incorrect because vision aids, such as binoculars, may be used only momentarily to enhance situational awareness. Answer (C) is incorrect because crewmembers must be able to see the sUAS at all times during flight.

Operating Limitations

The sUAS must be operated in accordance with the following limitations:

- Cannot be flown faster than a ground speed of 87 knots (100 miles per hour).

- Cannot be flown higher than 400 feet above ground level (AGL) unless flown within a 400-foot radius of a structure and not flown higher than 400 feet above the structure's immediate uppermost limit. *See* Figure 1-1.

Continued

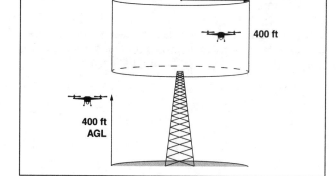

Figure 1-1. Flying near a tower

Crewmembers must operate within the following limitations:

- Minimum visibility, as observed from the location of the control station, must be no less than 3 statute miles.
- Minimum distance from clouds must be no less than 500 feet below a cloud and 2,000 feet horizontally from the cloud.

Note: These operating limitations are intended, among other things, to support the remote pilot's ability to identify hazardous conditions relating to encroaching aircraft or persons on the ground, and to take the appropriate actions to maintain safety.

1043. In accordance with 14 CFR Part 107, except when within a 400' radius of a structure, at what maximum altitude can you operate sUAS?

A— 600 feet AGL.
B— 500 feet AGL.
C— 400 feet AGL.

The sUAS cannot be flown higher than 400 feet above ground level (AGL) unless flown within a 400-foot radius of a structure and is not flown higher than 400 feet above the structure's immediate uppermost limit. (PLT373) — 14 CFR §107.51

1044. What speed limit applies to sUAS operations?

A— 200 knots.
B— 80 mph.
C— 100 mph.

The sUAS cannot be flown faster than a ground speed of 87 knots (100 miles per hour). (PLT373) — 14 CFR §107.51

1045. Unless otherwise authorized, what is the maximum airspeed at which a person may operate an sUAS below 400 feet?

A— 200 knots.
B— 80 mph.
C— 100 mph.

The sUAS cannot be flown faster than a ground speed of 87 knots (100 miles per hour) and must be operated below 400 feet. (PLT373) — 14 CFR §107.51

1046. The basic weather minimums for operating an sUAS up to the 400 feet AGL limit are

A— 900-foot ceiling and 3 mile visibility.
B— 2,000-foot ceiling and 1 miles visibility.
C— clear of clouds and 2 miles visibility.

Part 107 sUAS operations require minimum visibility of 3 SM and the minimum distance from clouds must be no less than 500 feet below the cloud; and 2,000 feet horizontally from the cloud. To maintain 500 feet below the clouds, you must have a 900-foot ceiling to be able to operate to the maximum 400 feet AGL, or a ceiling that would allow the sUAS to operate at a lower AGL altitude. (PLT527) — 14 CFR §107.51

1270. In accordance with 14 CFR Part 107, at what maximum altitude can you operate an sUAS when inspecting a tower with a top at 1,000 feet AGL at close proximity (within 100 feet)?

A— 1,400 feet MSL.
B— 1,400 feet AGL.
C— 400 feet AGL.

The sUAS cannot be flown higher than 400 feet AGL unless flown within a 400-foot radius of a structure and is not flown higher than 400 feet above the structure's immediate uppermost limit. (PLT373) — 14 CFR §107.51

Right-of-Way Rules

No person may operate a small unmanned aircraft in a manner that interferes with operations and traffic patterns at any airport, heliport, or seaplane base. The remote PIC also has a responsibility to remain clear of and yield right-of-way to all other aircraft, manned or unmanned, and avoid other potential hazards that may affect the remote PIC's operation of the aircraft. This is traditionally referred to as "see and avoid."

To satisfy this responsibility, the remote PIC must:

- Know the location and flight path of his or her small unmanned aircraft at all times.
- Be aware of other aircraft, persons, and property in the vicinity of the operating area.
- Be able to maneuver the small unmanned aircraft to:
  - Avoid a collision.
  - Prevent other aircraft from having to take evasive action.
- Avoid operating anywhere where the presence of his or her unmanned aircraft may interfere with operations at the airport, such as approach corridors, taxiways, runways, or helipads.
- Yield right-of-way to all other aircraft, including aircraft operating on the surface of the airport.

First-person view camera cannot satisfy the "see-and-avoid" requirement. However, such cameras can be used as long as the "see-and-avoid" requirement is satisfied in other ways, such as using visual observers.

1047. Which aircraft has right-of-way over the other traffic?

A— An airplane.
B— An sUAS.
C— A quadcopter.

The remote pilot operating an sUAS must yield right-of-way to all manned aircraft, including aircraft operating on the surface of the airport. (PLT414) — 14 CFR §107.37

1048. What action should the pilots take if a collision is anticipated?

A— The manned aircraft pilot should give way to the right.
B— The remote pilot should adjust the sUAS course.
C— Both pilots should give way to the right.

The remote PIC must be able to maneuver the sUAS to avoid a collision and prevent other aircraft from having to take evasive action. (PLT414) — 14 CFR §107.37

1049. What may be used to assist compliance with sUAS see-and-avoid requirements?

A— Binoculars.
B— First-person view camera.
C— remote pilot diligence.

The remote PIC also has a responsibility to remain clear of and yield right-of-way to all other aircraft, manned or unmanned, and avoid other potential hazards that may affect the remote PIC's operation of the aircraft. (PLT414) — 14 CFR §107.37

Answer (A) is incorrect because binoculars may be used only momentarily to enhance situational awareness. Answer (B) is incorrect because the first-person view camera cannot satisfy "see-and-avoid" requirement.

Answers

1047 [A]	1048 [B]	1049 [C]

No Operation Over People

You may not operate a small unmanned aircraft directly over another person unless that person is:

• Directly involved in the operation (such as a VO or other crewmember); or

• Within a safe cover, such as inside a stationary vehicle or a protective structure that would protect a person from harm if the small unmanned aircraft were to crash into that structure.

To comply with limitations on sUAS operations near persons not participating in the operation, the remote PIC should employ the strategies described below.

• Select an appropriate operational area for the sUAS flight:

— Ideally, select an operational area (site) that is sparsely populated.

— If operating in populated/inhabited areas, make a plan to keep non-participants clear, indoors, or under cover.

— If operating from a moving vehicle, choose a sparsely populated (or unpopulated) area and make a plan to keep sUAS clear of anyone who may approach.

• Adopt an appropriate operating distance from non-participants.

• Take reasonable precautions to keep the operational area free of non-participants.

1050. Which action is specifically required of the remote pilot prior to each flight?

A— Check the aircraft logbooks to ensure maintenance is current.

B— Make a plan to keep non-participants clear, indoors, or under cover.

C— Identify a non-participant who will be near the sUAS operation to help with see-and-avoid procedures.

You may not operate a small unmanned aircraft directly over another person unless that person is directly involved in the operation (such as a visual observer or other crewmember) or within a safe cover, such as inside a stationary vehicle or a protective structure that would protect a person from harm if the small unmanned aircraft were to crash into that structure. If operating in populated/inhabited areas, make a plan to keep non-participants clear, indoors, or under cover. (PLT373) — 14 CFR §107.39

1051. Remote pilots are required to complete the following operational area surveillance prior to a sUAS flight:

A— Select an operational area that is populated.

B— Make a plan to keep non-participants in viewing distance for the whole operation.

C— Keep the operational area free of and at an appropriate distance from all non-participants.

You may not operate a small unmanned aircraft directly over another person unless that person is directly involved in the operation (such as a VO or other crewmember) or within a safe cover, such as inside a stationary vehicle or a protective structure that would protect a person from harm if the small unmanned aircraft were to crash into that structure. (PLT373) — 14 CFR §107.39

1052. Except when necessary for takeoff or landing, what is the minimum safe altitude required for a remote pilot to operate an sUAS over people?

A— An altitude allowing, if a power unit fails, an emergency landing without undue hazard to persons or property on the surface.

B— An altitude of 200 feet above the highest obstacle within a horizontal radius of 1,000 feet.

C— You may not operate an sUAS over people who are not part of the sUAS operation.

You may not operate a small unmanned aircraft directly over another person unless that person is directly involved in the operation (such as a VO or other crewmember) or within a safe cover, such as inside a stationary vehicle or a protective structure that would protect a person from harm if the small unmanned aircraft were to crash into that structure. (PLT373) — 14 CFR §107.39

Answers

1050 [B]   1051 [C]   1052 [C]

Operation from Moving Vehicles or Aircraft

14 CFR Part 107 permits operation of an sUAS from a moving land or water-borne vehicle over a sparsely populated (or unpopulated) area. However, operation from a moving aircraft is prohibited. Additionally, small unmanned aircraft that are transporting another person's property for compensation or hire may not be operated from any moving vehicle.

Operations from moving vehicles are subject to the same restrictions that apply to all other Part 107 sUAS operations. Examples include:

- VLOS—the remote PIC (and the person manipulating the controls, if applicable) operating from a moving vehicle or watercraft is still required to maintain VLOS for the sUAS.

- Operations over people—operations are still prohibited over persons not directly involved in the operation of the sUAS, unless under safe cover. The remote PIC is also responsible for ensuring that no person is subject to undue risk as a result of loss of control of the small unmanned aircraft for any reason.

- Communication—the visual observer and remote PIC must still maintain effective communication.

- No reckless operation—Part 107 also prohibits careless or reckless operation of an sUAS. Operating an sUAS while driving a moving vehicle is considered to be careless or reckless because the driver's attention would be hazardously divided. Therefore, the driver of a land vehicle or the operator of a waterborne vehicle must not serve as the remote PIC, person manipulating the controls, or visual observer. As another example, failure to consider weather conditions near structures, trees, or rolling terrain when operating in a densely populated area could be determined as careless or reckless operation.

Other laws, such as state and local traffic laws, may also apply to the conduct of a person driving a vehicle. Many states currently prohibit distracted driving and state or local laws may also be amended in the future to impose restrictions on how cars and public roads may be used with regard to an sUAS operation. The FAA emphasizes that people involved in an sUAS operation are responsible for complying with all applicable laws and not just the FAA's regulations.

1053. A professional wildlife photographer operates an sUAS from a moving truck to capture aerial images of migrating birds in remote wetlands. The driver of the truck does not serve any crewmember role in the operation. Is this sUAS operation in compliance with 14 CFR Part 107?

A— Compliant with Part 107.
B— Not compliant with Part 107.
C— Not compliant with state and local traffic laws.

You may operate an sUAS from a moving vehicle if you are in a sparsely populated area and the driver does not serve as the remote PIC, person manipulating the controls, or visual observer. (PLT373) — 14 CFR §107.25

1054. In accordance with 14 CFR Part 107, you may operate an sUAS from a moving vehicle when no property is carried for compensation or hire

A— over suburban areas.
B— over a parade or other social event.
C— over a sparsely populated area.

Operation of an sUAS is permitted from a moving land or waterborne vehicle over a sparsely populated (or unpopulated) area. (PLT373) — 14 CFR §107.25

Answers
1053 [A]   1054 [C]

1055. Which of the following operations is compliant with 14 CFR Part 107?

A— Remote PIC is driving a moving vehicle while operating an sUAS in a sparsely populated area.

B— Remote PIC is a passenger on an aircraft in flight while operating an sUAS.

C— Remote PIC is a passenger in a moving boat while operating an sUAS in an unpopulated area.

Operation of an sUAS is permitted from a moving land or waterborne vehicle over a sparsely populated (or unpopulated) area. (PLT373) — 14 CFR §107.25

Privacy and Other Considerations

No person may operate an sUAS in a careless or reckless manner that would endanger another person's life or property. Part 107 also prohibits allowing an object to be dropped from an sUAS in a way that causes undue hazard to persons or property. Examples of hazardous operation include, but are not limited to:

- Operations that interfere with manned aircraft operations.
- Operating an sUAS over persons not directly participating in the operation.
- Loading the sUAS beyond its capabilities to the point of losing control.

You may operate an sUAS to transport another person's property (cargo) for compensation or hire provided you comply with the additional requirements described below:

- The total weight of the sUAS (including the cargo) must remain below 55 pounds.
- The sUAS operation must be within the boundaries of a State (intrastate).
- No items may be dropped from the small unmanned aircraft in a manner that creates undue hazard to persons or property.
- You may not operate the sUAS from a moving land vehicle or waterborne vessel.
- Carriage of hazardous materials is not permitted.

As with other operations in Part 107, sUAS operations involving the transport of property must be conducted within VLOS of the remote pilot. While the VLOS limitation can be waived for some operations under the rule, it cannot be waived for transportation of property. Additionally, Part 107 does not allow the operation of an sUAS from a moving vehicle or aircraft if the small UA is being used to transport property for compensation or hire. This limitation cannot be waived. Additionally, the remote pilot must know the sUAS location in order to determine the attitude, altitude, and direction; to yield the right-of-way to other aircraft; and to maintain the ability to see and avoid other aircraft.

Other laws, such as State and local privacy laws, may apply to sUAS operations. The remote PIC is responsible for reviewing and complying with such laws prior to operation.

In addition, remote PICs are encouraged to review the Department of Commerce National Telecommunications and Information Administration (NTIA) best practices, which address privacy, transparency and accountability issues related to private and commercial use of sUAS.

Answers

1055 [C]

1056. Personnel at an outdoor concert venue use an sUAS to drop promotional t-shirts and CDs over the audience. Is this sUAS operation in compliance with 14 CFR Part 107?

A— Yes, compliant with Part 107.
B— Not compliant with Part 107.
C— No, unless authorized by the venue.

This scenario is not compliant with Part 107. You may not operate over non-participants without safe cover and you may not drop objects in a manner that creates a hazard. (PLT401) — AC 107-2

1057. Under what conditions may objects be dropped from the sUAS?

A— In an emergency.
B— If precautions are taken to avoid injury or damage to persons or property on the surface.
C— If prior permission is received from the Federal Aviation Administration.

No items may be dropped from the small unmanned aircraft in a manner that creates undue hazard to persons or property. (PLT401) — 14 CFR §107.23

1058. You wish to start a local delivery business using an sUAS to drop small packages at the front door of customer. The customer's residence is not always within visual line-of-sight (VLOS) of the Remote PIC located at the delivery facility. Under which circumstances would this be authorized?

A— With a waiver from the FAA.
B— By utilizing a vehicle to follow the sUAS while enroute to maintain VLOS.
C— There is currently no way to do this in compliance with AC 107-2.

The FAA has stated that they will not provide waivers for beyond VLOS during the carriage of goods for hire. Also, moving vehicles (land or sea) are not authorized to be used during flights upon which goods are carried for hire. (PLT401) — AC 107-2

Answers (A) and (B) are incorrect because these are specifically prohibited per AC 107-2.

Alcohol and Drugs

Part 107 does not allow operation of an sUAS if the remote PIC, person manipulating the controls, or VO is unable to safely carry out his or her responsibilities. It is the remote PIC's responsibility to ensure all crewmembers are not participating in the operation while impaired. While drugs and alcohol use are known to impair judgment, certain over-the-counter (OTC) medications and medical conditions could also affect the ability to safely operate a small UA. For example, certain antihistamines and decongestants may cause drowsiness. Pilots can learn more about the impact of drugs and alcohol on flight operations in the *Pilot's Handbook of Aeronautical Knowledge* (FAA-H-8083-25).

Part 107 prohibits a person from serving as a remote PIC, person manipulating the controls, VO, or other crewmember if he or she:

• Consumed any alcoholic beverage within the preceding 8 hours;

• Is under the influence of alcohol;

• Has a blood alcohol concentration of .04 percent or greater; and/or

• Is using a drug that affects the person's mental or physical capabilities.

A refusal to submit to a test to indicate the percentage by weight of alcohol in the blood, when requested by a law enforcement officer, or a refusal to furnish or authorize the release of the test results requested by the Administrator, is grounds for:

Continued

Answers
1056 [B]   1057 [B]   1058 [C]

- Denial of an application for a remote pilot certificate with a small UAS rating for a period of up to 1 year after the date of that refusal; or
- Suspension or revocation of a remote pilot certificate with a small UAS rating.

Certain medical conditions, such as epilepsy, may also create a risk to operations. It is the remote PIC's responsibility to determine that their medical condition is under control and they can safely conduct a UAS operation.

1059. Who holds the responsibility to ensure all crewmembers who are participating in the operation are not impaired by drugs or alcohol?

A— Remote pilot in command.
B— The FAA.
C— Site supervisor.

The remote PIC or person manipulating the flight controls of an sUAS must comply with the "do not operate while impaired" regulations. (PLT463) — 14 CFR §§107.19 (b), 107.19 (d), and 107.57

1060. A person may not act as a crewmember of a sUAS if alcoholic beverages have been consumed by that person within the preceding

A— 8 hours.
B— 12 hours.
C— 24 hours.

No person may act or attempt to act as a crewmember of a sUAS within 8 hours after the consumption of any alcoholic beverage. Remember "8 hours bottle to throttle." (PLT463) — 14 CFR §§107.27 and 91.17

1061. No person may attempt to act as a crewmember of a sUAS with

A— .4 percent by weight or more alcohol in the blood.
B— .004 percent by weight or more alcohol in the blood.
C— .04 percent by weight or more alcohol in the blood.

No person may act, or attempt to act, as a crewmember of a civil aircraft while having .04 percent or more, by weight, alcohol in the blood. (PL463) — 14 CFR §§107.27 and 91.17

1062. Which is true regarding the presence of alcohol within the human body?

A— A small amount of alcohol increases vision acuity.
B— Consuming an equal amount of water will increase the destruction of alcohol and alleviate a hangover.
C— Judgment and decision-making abilities can be adversely affected by even small amounts of alcohol.

As little as one ounce of liquor, one bottle of beer, or four ounces of wine can impair flying skills. (PLT205) — AIM ¶8-1-1

Answer (A) is incorrect because all mental and physical activities will be decreased with even small amounts of alcohol in the bloodstream. Answer (B) is incorrect because water does not increase the metabolism of alcohol.

1063. A law enforcement officer witnesses careless or reckless behavior while observing sUAS operations and requests the operator submit to a drug or alcohol test. What are the consequences if this request is denied?

A— The operator may be denied an application for a remote pilot certificate for up to 30 days.
B— The operator may have to pay a fine but their remote pilot certificate will not be affected.
C— The operator may have their remote pilot certificate with sUAS rating suspended or revoked.

A refusal to submit to a test to indicate the percentage by weight of alcohol in the blood, when requested by a law enforcement officer, or a refusal to furnish or authorize the release of the test results requested by the Administrator, is grounds for denial of an application for a remote pilot certificate with a small UAS rating for a period of up to 1 year after the date of that refusal, or suspension or revocation of a remote pilot certificate with a small UAS rating. (PLT463) — 14 CFR §107.59

Answer (A) is incorrect because the remote pilot applicant could be denied application for up to 1 year after the date of refusal. Answer (B) is incorrect because the operator could risk having their remote pilot certificate suspended or revoked.

Answers

1059 [A]	1060 [A]	1061 [C]	1062 [C]	1063 [C]

1275. When can someone with a marijuana conviction apply for a Remote Pilot certificate?

A— Never.
B— 18 months.
C— 1 year.

A conviction for the violation of any Federal or State statute relating to the growing, processing, manufacture, sale, disposition, possession, transportation, or importation of narcotic drugs, marijuana, or depressant or stimulant drugs or substances is grounds for denial of an application for a remote pilot certificate with a small UAS rating for a period of up to 1 year after the date of that act. (PLT463) — 14 CFR §107.57

1306. If you are caught smoking marijuana the FAA will

A— Send you to a drug treatment center.
B— Issue an immediate suspension or revocation of your pilot certificate.
C— Deny all future pilot applications.

A conviction for the violation of any Federal or State statute relating to the growing, processing, manufacture, sale, disposition, possession, transportation, or importation of narcotic drugs, marijuana, or depressant or stimulant drugs or substances is grounds for suspension or revocation of a remote pilot certificate with a small UAS rating. (PLT463) — 14 CFR §107.57

1281. What FAA resource can pilots reference to learn more about the impact of drugs and alcohol on flight?

A— The *Pilot's Handbook of Aeronautical Knowledge.*
B— The Pilot Operating Handbook.
C— NOTAMs.

The Pilot's Handbook of Aeronautical Knowledge (FAA-H-8083-25) provides information on the physiological effects of alcohol, prescription drugs, and over-the-counter medications. (PLT529) — FAA-H-8083-25

Change of Address

If a remote pilot changes his or her permanent mailing address without notifying the FAA Airman's Certification Branch, in writing, within 30 days, then he or she may not exercise privileges of his or her certificate.

1064. If a certificated pilot changes permanent mailing address and fails to notify the FAA Airmen Certification Branch of the new address, the pilot is entitled to exercise the privileges of the pilot certificate for a period of only

A— 30 days after the date of the move.
B— 60 days after the date of the move.
C— 90 days after the date of the move.

The holder of a remote pilot certificate who has made a change in his/her permanent mailing address may not, after 30 days from the date moved, exercise the privileges of his/her certificate unless he/she has notified in writing the FAA Airman Certification Branch. (PLT387) — 14 CFR §107.77

Waivers

If the remote PIC determines that the operation cannot be conducted within the regulatory structure of Part 107, he or she is responsible for applying for a Certificate of Waiver (CoW) and proposing a safe alternative to the operation. This CoW will allow an sUAS operation to deviate from certain provisions of Part 107 as long as the FAA finds that the proposed operation can be safely conducted under the terms of that CoW.

The Part 107 sections which may be waived include:

- § 107.25 "Operation from a moving vehicle or aircraft. However, no waiver of this provision will be issued to allow the carriage of property of another by aircraft for compensation or hire."

- § 107.29 "Daylight operation."

Continued

Answers

1275 [C]   1306 [B]   1281 [A]   1064 [A]

- § 107.31 "Visual line of sight aircraft operation. However, no waiver of this provision will be issued to allow the carriage of property of another by aircraft for compensation or hire."
- § 107.33 "Visual observer."
- § 107.35 "Operation of multiple small unmanned aircraft systems."
- § 107.37(a) "Yielding the right of way."
- § 107.39 "Operation over people."
- § 107.41 "Operation in certain airspace."
- § 107.51 "Operating limitations for small unmanned aircraft."

After submitting your online CoW application, the FAA will determine if the proposed operation can be conducted safely. If the application is denied, you will receive notification stating the reasons for denial. If the waiver or authorization is granted, you will receive direct notification with:

- The completed FAA Form 7711-1, *Certificate of Waiver or Authorization*, dated, signed, and approved by the FAA; and
- Specific special provisions that become regulatory for the waiver holder.

1065. The FAA may approve your application for a waiver of provisions in Part 107 only when it has been determined that the proposed operation

A— involves public aircraft or air carrier operations.
B— can be safely conducted under the terms of that certificate of waiver.
C— will be conducted outside of the United States.

If the remote PIC determines that the operation cannot be conducted within the regulatory structure of Part 107, he or she is responsible for applying for a Certificate of Waiver (CoW) and proposing a safe alternative to the operation. This CoW will allow an sUAS operation to deviate from certain provisions of Part 107 as long as the FAA finds that the proposed operation can be safely conducted under the terms of that Certificate of Waiver. (PLT373) — 14 CFR §107.200

Answers (A) and (C) are incorrect because these operations fall outside the regulatory scope of Part 107.

1066. When requesting a waiver, the required documents should be presented to the FAA at least how many days prior to the planned operation?

A— 30 days.
B— 10 days.
C— 90 days.

Although not required by Part 107, the FAA encourages applicants to submit their application at least 90 days prior to the start of the proposed operation. The FAA will strive to complete review and adjudication of waivers within 90 days; however, the time required for the FAA to make a determination regarding waiver requests will vary based on the complexity of the request. (PLT373) — AC 107-2

Answers
1065 [B]   1066 [C]

Chapter 2
National Airspace System

Introduction

The remote pilot certificate with an sUAS rating will allow operation of an sUAS in the **National Airspace System (NAS)**. There are two categories of airspace or airspace areas: Regulatory (Class A, B, C, D and E airspace areas, restricted, and prohibited areas) and nonregulatory (Class G airspace, military operations areas, warning areas, alert areas, and controlled firing areas). Class A, B, C, D, and E airspace areas are referred to as **controlled airspace** and Class G airspace areas are referred to as **uncontrolled airspace**. You must become familiar with the NAS in order to safely operate with the others sharing this airspace, as well as with the nonparticipants on the ground. The following resources are critical for remote PICs to be able to understand airspace and the NAS, as well as invaluable tools for adequately planning safe operations in compliance with regulations and restrictions.

Refer to the *Chart Supplement U.S.* (formerly the *Airport/Facility Directory* or A/FD) to determine what kind of airspace, air traffic control facilities, and traffic you can expect near the airport closest to your operations. The *Chart Supplement U.S.* is a publication for pilots containing key information about all airports, seaplane bases, and heliports open to the public including communications data, navigational facilities, and certain special notices and procedures. This supplement is reissued in its entirety every 56 days. *See* CT-8080-2X, Figure 31 for a sample *Chart Supplement U.S.*

The aeronautical map most commonly used by manned pilots are the Sectional Aeronautical Chart and the Terminal Area Chart (TAC). Both charts include aeronautical information such as airports, airways, special use airspace, and other pertinent data. These charts are of tremendous value to the remote pilot operating an sUAS. The scale of the Sectional Aeronautical Chart is 1:500,000 (1 inch = 6.86 NM). Designed for visual navigation of slow speed aircraft in visual conditions (referred to as VFR), this chart portrays terrain relief and checkpoints such as populated places, roads, railroads, and other distinctive landmarks. These charts are revised every 6 months. *See* CT-8080-2X, Legend 1 to become familiar with the Sectional Chart Legend, and Figure 20 on page A-4 for a sample Sectional excerpt. Information found on the TAC is similar to that found on the Sectional Chart, but at a scale of 1:250,000 (1 inch = 3.43 NM). These charts display a specific city with Class B airspace. They show more significant detail than the Sectional Chart, but have small area coverage.

NOTAMs

Notices to Airmen (NOTAMs) provide the most current information available and can be found by visiting **www.faa.gov**, or obtained from the FAA's Flight Service by referencing **www.1800wxbrief.com**. Also, Air Traffic Publications generates the *Notices to Airmen Publication* (NTAP) every 28 days that contains all current NOTAM (D)s and FDC NOTAMs (except FDC NOTAMs for temporary flight restrictions) available for publication. They provide time-critical information on airports and changes that affect the NAS. It is necessary for the sUAS remote PIC to check for NOTAMs before each flight to determine if there are any applicable airspace restrictions.

NOTAM information is classified into four categories: NOTAM (D) or "distant," Flight Data Center (FDC) NOTAMs, pointer NOTAMs, and military NOTAMs. In addition to being available from flight service stations (FSS), NOTAM (D)s are transmitted with hourly weather reports. FDC NOTAMs are issued by the National Flight Data Center (NFDC) and contain regulatory information such as temporary flight restrictions or an amendment to instrument approach procedures. Pointer NOTAMs highlight or point out another NOTAM, such as the issuance of an FDC or NOTAM (D). This type of NOTAM will assist pilots in cross-referencing important information that might not be found under an airport or NAVAID identifier. Military NOTAMs pertain to U.S. Air Force, Army, Navy and Marine NAVAIDs/airports that are part of the NAS. NOTAM (D)s and FDC NOTAMs are contained in the Notices to Airmen publication, which is issued every 28 days. Prior to any flight, all types of pilots must check for any NOTAMs that could affect their intended flight.

Continued

An FDC NOTAM will be issued to designate a temporary flight restriction (TFR). The NOTAM will begin with the phrase "FLIGHT RESTRICTIONS" followed by the location of the temporary restriction, effective time period, area defined in statute miles, and altitudes affected. The NOTAM will also contain the FAA coordination facility and telephone number, the reason for the restriction, and any other information deemed appropriate. TFRs are inclusive of sUAS operations; therefore it is necessary for the remote PIC to check for NOTAMs before each flight to determine if there are any applicable airspace restrictions. Common TFRs that relate to sUAS operations include, but are not limited to:

- Presidential TFRs and NOTAMs (e.g., when the President, or other important public figures are travelling or at a specific location).
- Emergency response TFRs and NOTAMs (e.g., forest fires and other disasters).
- Standing TFRs that go into and out of effect (e.g., stadiums for sporting events)

  TFRs may also be found at the FAA website: **http://tfr.faa.gov**.

Other Airspace Resources

Additional resources on the subject of airspace include ACs and the AIM. ACs are issued systematically by the FAA to inform the aviation community of non-regulatory material of interest. In many cases, they are the result of a need to fully explain a particular subject (the pilot's role in collision avoidance, for example). They are issued in a numbered-subject system corresponding to the subject areas of the Federal Aviation Regulations. ACs are available from **www.faa.gov** and are also occasionally issued in print for a fee. Some ACs include additional information on airspace. The AIM is the official guide to basic flight information and ATC procedures, which is issued yearly with ongoing revisions. These resources should be reviewed by remote PICs.

1067. The most comprehensive information on a given airport is provided by

A— the *Chart Supplement U.S.* (formerly *Airport/ Facility Directory*).
B— Notices to Airmen (NOTAMs).
C— Terminal Area Chart (TAC).

The Chart Supplement U.S. is a publication for pilots containing information about airports, seaplane bases, and heliports open to the public including communications data, navigational facilities, and certain special notices and procedures. (PLT281) — FAA-H-8083-25

Answers (B) and (C) are incorrect because these publications do not have comprehensive and specific airport information.

1068. (Refer to Figure 20, area 5.) How would a remote PIC "CHECK NOTAMS" as noted in the CAUTION box regarding the unmarked balloon?

A— By utilizing the B4UFLY mobile application.
B— By contacting the FAA district office.
C— By obtaining a briefing via an online source such as 1800WXbrief.com.

*Notices to Airmen (NOTAMs) provide the most current information available and can be found by visiting **www. faa.gov** or obtained at a flight service station (FSS). A comprehensive weather briefing can be obtained as part of a standard preflight briefing. (PLT323) — FAA-H-8083-25*

1313. An FDC NOTAM will typically contain information

A— regarding public gatherings of large groups.
B— regarding military operations.
C— regarding available hard surface runways.

Notices to Airmen (NOTAMs) provide time-critical aeronautical information either temporary in nature or not sufficiently known in advance to permit publication on aeronautical charts or in other operational publications. (PLT323) — FAA-H-8083-25

Answers

1067 [A]   1068 [C]   1313 [A]

1069. What information is contained in the *Notices to Airman Publication* (NTAP)?

A— Current NOTAM (D) and FDC NOTAMs.
B— All Current NOTAMs.
C— Current FDC NOTAMs.

The Notices to Airmen Publication (NTAP) is published by Air Traffic Publications every 28 days and contains all current NOTAM (D)s and FDC NOTAMs (except FDC NOTAMs for TFRs) available for publication. (PLT323) — FAA-H-8083-25

1070. Flight Data Center (FDC) NOTAMS are issued by the National Flight Data Center and contain regulatory information, such as

A— temporary flight restrictions.
B— markings and signs used at airports.
C— standard communication procedures at uncontrolled airports.

FDC NOTAMs are issued by the National Flight Data Center and contain regulatory information, such as Temporary Flight Restrictions. (PLT323) — FAA-H-8083-25

1071. Time-critical information on airports and changes that affect the national airspace system are provided by

A— Notices to Airmen (NOTAMS).
B— The *Chart Supplement U.S.* (formerly *Airport/ Facilities Directory* or A/FD).
C— Advisory Circulars (ACs).

Notices to Airmen (NOTAMs) provide the most current information available. They provide time-critical information on airports and changes that affect the NAS. (PLT323) — FAA-H-8083-25

Answer (B) is incorrect because the Chart Supplement U.S. is only revised every 8 weeks. Answer (C) is incorrect because the FAA systematically issues ACs to inform the aviation public of nonregulatory material.

1072. One of the purposes for issuing a temporary flight restriction (TFR) is to

A— announce Parachute Jump Areas.
B— protect public figures.
C— identify Airport Advisory Areas.

TFRs are imposed in order to:

1. *Protect persons and property in the air or on the surface from an existing or imminent flight associated hazard;*

2. *Provide a safe environment for the operation of disaster relief aircraft;*

3. *Prevent an unsafe congestion of sightseeing aircraft above an incident;*

4. *Protect the President, Vice President, or other public figures; and,*

5. *Provide a safe environment for space agency operations.*

Pilots are expected to check appropriate NOTAMs during flight planning when conducting flight in an area where a TFR is in effect. (PLT376) — FAA-H-8083-25

Answer (A) is incorrect because this is done through NOTAMs. Answer (C) is incorrect because these are identified through the sectional and Chart Supplement U.S.

1073. Public figures are protected by

A— special use airspace.
B— prohibited areas.
C— temporary flight restrictions.

TFRs are imposed in order to:

1. *Protect persons and property in the air or on the surface from an existing or imminent flight associated hazard;*

2 *Provide a safe environment for the operation of disaster relief aircraft;*

3. *Prevent an unsafe congestion of sightseeing aircraft above an incident;*

4. *Protect the President, Vice President, or other public figures; and,*

5. *Provide a safe environment for space agency operations.*

Pilots are expected to check appropriate NOTAMs during flight planning when conducting flight in an area where a TFR is in effect. (PLT376) — FAA-H-8083-25

Answer (A) is incorrect because special use airspace is the broad category to include alert, controlled firing, military operations, prohibited, restricted, and warning areas; none of these are used to protect public figures. Answer (B) is incorrect because prohibited areas are blocks of airspace within which the flight of all aircraft is prohibited.

1074. The FAA publication that provides the aviation community with basic flight information and Air Traffic Control procedures for use in the National Airspace System of the United States is the

A— Aeronautical Information Manual (AIM).
B— *Chart Supplement U.S.* (formerly A/FD).
C— *Advisory Circular Checklist* (AC 00-2).

The Aeronautical Information Manual (AIM) is the official guide to basic flight information and ATC procedures. (PLT116) — AIM

Answer (B) is incorrect because the Chart Supplement U.S. contains information on airports and various other pertinent special notices essential to operating in the NAS. Answer (C) is incorrect because AC 00-2 is the Advisory Circular Checklist for the status of all other FAA publications.

1075. (Refer to Figure 31.) Within what airspace is Coeur D'Alene Pappy Boyington Fld located?

A— Class B.
B— Class E.
C— Class D.

The Chart Supplement U.S. includes airport details, including the airspace the airport lies in. Figure 31 shows Coeur D'Alene airport lies within Class E airspace. (PLT161) — Chart Supplement U.S.

1076. (Refer to Figure 52.) What special conditions do remote pilots need to be on the lookout for while operating near Lincoln Airport?

A— Deer near the runway.
B— Birds in the vicinity.
C— Parachute operations.

The Chart Supplement U.S. includes airport details, including remarks unique to that airport. Figure 52 shows an abbreviated remark for Lincoln Airport, "Birds invof aipt." (PLT281) — Chart Supplement U.S.

1276. Checking the NOTAMs confirms the Blue Angels are scheduled to perform at the local airport. When can UAS operations resume relative to this NOTAM?

A— Once the Blue Angels have landed.
B— With ATC authorization.
C— Immediately, so long as a 1 NM distance is maintained.

A NOTAM may be issued for reasons including hazards, such as air shows. The NOTAM will include the location and time for the affected region. UAS operations should stay away from these locations during the timeframe defined by the NOTAM. (PLT323) — FAA-H-8083-25

Airspace Classification

It is very important that sUAS remote PICs be aware of the type of airspace in which they will be operating their small UA. Referring to the "B4UFly" app, or a current aeronautical chart (**http://faacharts.faa.gov**) of the intended operating area will aid a remote PIC's decision-making regarding sUAS operations in the NAS.

Though many sUAS operations will occur in uncontrolled airspace, there are some that may need to operate in controlled airspace. Operations in what is called controlled airspace, i.e. Class B, Class C, or Class D airspace, or within the lateral boundaries of the surface area of Class E airspace designated for an airport, are not allowed unless that person has prior authorization from ATC.

The sUAS remote PIC must understand airspace classifications and requirements. The authorization process can be found at **www.faa.gov/uas**. Although sUAS will not be subject to Part 91, the equipage and communications requirements outlined in Part 91 were designed to provide safety and efficiency in controlled airspace. Accordingly, while sUAS operating under Part 107 are not subject to Part 91, as a practical matter, ATC authorization or clearance may depend on operational parameters similar to those found in Part 91. The FAA has the authority to approve or deny aircraft operations based on traffic density, controller workload, communication issues, or any other type of operations that could potentially impact the safe and expeditious flow of air traffic in that airspace. Those planning sUAS operations in controlled airspace are encouraged to contact the FAA as early as possible.

Many sUAS operations can be conducted in uncontrolled, Class G airspace without further permission or authorization. However, controlled airspace operations require prior authorization from ATC and there-

Answers

1074 [A]   1075 [B]   1076 [B]   1276 [A]

fore it is incumbent on the remote PIC to be aware of the type of airspace in which they will be operating their sUAS. As with other flight operations, the remote PIC should refer to current aeronautical charts and other navigation tools to determine position and related airspace.

Controlled airspace, that is, airspace within which some or all aircraft may be subject to air traffic control, consists of those areas designated as Class A, Class B, Class C, Class D, and Class E airspace. Much of the controlled airspace begins at either 700 feet or 1,200 feet above the ground. The lateral limits and floors of Class E airspace of 700 feet are defined by a magenta vignette (shading) on the Sectional Chart; while the lateral limits and floors of 1,200 feet are defined by a blue vignette on the Sectional Chart if it abuts uncontrolled airspace. Floors other than 700 feet or 1,200 feet are indicated by a number indicating the floor. *See* Figure 2-1.

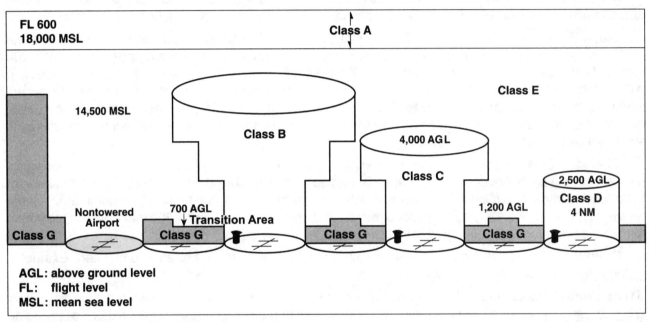

Figure 2-1. National Airspace System: airspace classification

Class A—Class A airspace extends from 18,000 feet MSL (mean sea level) up to and including Flight Level (FL) 600 (60,000 feet) and is not depicted on VFR sectional charts. No flight under visual flight rules (VFR) is authorized in Class A airspace.

Class B—Class B airspace consists of controlled airspace extending upward from the surface or higher up to specified altitudes. Class B airspace size, altitudes, and layouts vary greatly from one site to another which are centered around one or more primary airports. Each Class B airspace sector, outlined in blue on the Sectional Chart, is labeled with its delimiting arcs, radials, and altitudes. Within each segment, the floor and ceiling are denoted by one number over a second number or the letters SFC. Class B airspace is also depicted on the Terminal Area Chart; on these each Class B airspace sector is, again, outlined in blue and is labeled with its delimiting arcs, radials, and altitudes. An ATC clearance is required prior to operating within Class B airspace. Some large, very busy airports are designated as Class B Primary airports; these require the pilot hold at least a Private Pilot certificate and may have additional operating requirements or limitations.

Class C—All Class C airspace shares the same dimensions with minor site variations. Class C is composed of two circles, both centered on the primary airport. The inner surface area has a radius of 5 nautical miles (NM) and extends from the surface up to 4,000 feet above the airport. The "outer shelf" area has a radius of 10 NM and extends vertically from 1,200 feet AGL (above ground level) up to 4,000 feet above the primary airport. In addition to the Class C airspace proper, there is an outer area with a

Continued

radius of 20 NM that has vertical coverage from the lower limits of the radio/radar coverage up to the top of the approach control facility's delegated airspace. Within the outer area, pilots are encouraged to participate but it is not a requirement. Class C airspace service to aircraft proceeding to a satellite airport is terminated at a sufficient distance to allow time to change to the appropriate tower or advisory frequency. On aeronautical charts, Class C airspace is depicted by solid magenta lines. Class C requires two-way radio communications equipment, a transponder, and an encoding altimeter.

Class D—Class D airspace extends upward from the surface to approximately 2,500 feet AGL (the actual height is as needed). Class D airspace may include one or more airports and is normally 4 NM in radius centered around a designated airport. The actual size and shape is depicted on sectional charts by a blue dashed line and numbers showing the top or airspace ceiling. When the ceiling of Class D airspace is less than 1,000 feet and/or the visibility is less than 3 statute miles, additional restrictions exist for manned aircraft and may preclude UAS operations; contact ATC for information during these circumstances.

Class E—Magenta shading on the Sectional Chart identifies Class E airspace starting at 700 feet AGL, and no shading (or blue if next to Class G airspace) identifies Class E airspace starting at 1,200 feet AGL. It may also start at other altitudes. All airspace from 14,500 feet to 17,999 feet is Class E airspace. It also includes the surface area of some airports with an instrument approach but no control tower. An airway is a corridor of Class E airspace extending from 1,200 feet above the surface (or as designated) up to and including 17,999 feet MSL, and 4 NM either side of the centerline. The airway is indicated by a centerline, shown in blue.

Class G—Class G airspace is airspace within which ATC has neither the authority nor responsibility to exercise any control over air traffic. Class G airspace typically extends from the surface to the base of the overlying controlled (Class E) airspace, which is normally 700 or 1,200 feet AGL. In some areas of the western U.S. and Alaska, Class G airspace may extend from the surface to 14,500 feet MSL. An exception to this rule occurs when 14,500 feet MSL is lower than 1,500 feet AGL.

Prohibited Areas are blocks of airspace within which the flight of aircraft is prohibited. Examples include the airspace around the White House and the U.S. Capitol building.

Restricted Areas denote the presence of unusual, often invisible, hazards to aircraft such as artillery firing, aerial gunnery, or guided missiles. Penetration of restricted areas without authorization of the using or controlling agency may be extremely hazardous to the aircraft and its occupants. Per 14 CFR Part 107, entry into restricted airspace is not authorized without permission from the controlling agency.

Warning Areas contain the same hazardous activities as those found in restricted areas, but are located in international airspace. Prohibited, restricted, or warning areas are depicted as shown in CT-8080-2X, Legend 1.

Military Operations Areas (MOAs) consist of airspace established for the purpose of separating certain military training activities from instrument flight rules (IFR) traffic. Pilots should exercise extreme caution while flying within an active MOA. Prior to entering an active MOA, pilots should contact the controlling agency for traffic advisories.

Alert Areas may contain a high volume of pilot training activities or an unusual type of aerial activity. Pilots should be particularly alert when flying in these areas. Pilots of participating aircraft as well as pilots transiting the area are equally responsible for collision avoidance.

FAA Advisory Circular AC 91-36, *Visual Flight Rules (VFR) Flight Near Noise-Sensitive Areas*, defines the surface of a national park area (including parks, forests, primitive areas, wilderness areas, recreational areas, national seashores, national monuments, national lakeshores, and national wildlife refuge and range areas) as: the highest terrain within 2,000 feet laterally of the route of flight, or the upper-most rim of a canyon or valley. These are marked on sectional charts with a solid blue line on the outside of the area border with blue dots on the inside of the border line. Aircraft are requested to remain at least 2,000 feet above the surface of National Parks, National Monuments, Wilderness and Primitive Areas, and National Wildlife Refuges.

Local Airport Advisory (LAA) is an advisory service provided by Flight Service facilities, which are located on the landing airport, using a discrete ground-to-air frequency or the tower frequency when the tower is closed. LAA services include local airport advisories, automated weather reporting with voice broadcasting, and a continuous Automated Surface Observing System (ASOS)/Automated Weather Observing Station (AWOS) data display, other continuous direct reading instruments, or manual observations available to the specialist.

Military Training Routes (MTRs) have been developed for use by the military for the purpose of conducting low-altitude, high-speed training. Generally, MTRs are established below 10,000 feet MSL for operations at speeds in excess of 250 knots. IFR Military Training Route (IR) operations are conducted in accordance with instrument flight rules, regardless of weather conditions. VFR Military Training Routes (VR) operations are conducted in accordance with visual flight rules. IR and VR at and below 1,500 feet AGL (with no segment above 1,500) will be identified by four digit numbers, e.g. VR1351, IR1007. IR and VR with one or more segments above 1,500 AGL (routes can be above or below 1,500 feet AGL will be identified by three digit numbers, e.g. IR341, VR426. The lateral boundaries of MTRs vary. For more information, pilots should consult the Department of Defense Flight Information Publication (FLIP).

When ATC authorization is required (at or near an airport with a control tower and/or when operating within controlled airspace), it must be requested and granted before any operation in that airspace. There is currently no established timeline for approval after ATC permission has been requested because the time required for approval will vary based on the resources available at the ATC facility and the complexity and safety issues raised by each specific request. For this reason, remote PICs should contact the appropriate ATC facility as soon as possible prior to any operation in Class B, C and D airspace and within the lateral boundaries of the surface area of Class E airspace designated for an airport. ATC has the authority to approve or deny aircraft operations based on traffic density, controller workload, communication issues, or any other type of operations that could potentially impact the safe and expeditious flow of air traffic in that airspace.

When ATC authorization is not required (at or near an airport without a control tower and/or when operating within uncontrolled airspace), remote pilots should monitor the Common Traffic Advisory Frequency (CTAF) of any nearby airport(s)to stay aware of manned aircraft communications and operations. The CTAF can be found in the *Chart Supplement U.S.* and on Sectional and Terminal Area Charts (noted by a magenta "C" next to the frequency).

1077. (Refer to Figure 25, area 4.) The floor of Class B airspace overlying Hicks Airport (T67) north-northwest of Fort Worth Meacham Field is

A— at the surface.
B— 3,200 feet MSL.
C— 4,000 feet MSL.

The thick blue lines on the sectional chart indicate the boundaries of the overlying Class B airspace. Within each segment, the floor and ceiling are denoted by one number over a second number or the letters SFC. The floor of the Class B airspace is 4,000 feet MSL. (PLT040) — AIM ¶3-2-3

1078. (Refer to Figure 23, area 3.) What is the floor of the Savannah Class C airspace at the shelf area (outer circle)?

A— 1,300 feet AGL.
B— 1,300 feet MSL.
C— 1,700 feet MSL.

Within the outer magenta circle of Savannah Class C airspace, there is a number 41 directly above the number 13. These numbers depict the floor and ceiling of the Class C airspace; the floor being 1,300 feet MSL and the ceiling being 4,100 feet MSL. (PLT040) — AIM ¶3-2-4

Answers

1077 [C]   1078 [B]

1079. According to 14 CFR Part 107, the remote PIC of a small unmanned aircraft planning to operate within Class C airspace

A— is required to receive ATC authorization.
B— is required to file a flight plan.
C— must use a visual observer.

No person may operate a small unmanned aircraft in Class B, Class C, or Class D airspace or within the lateral boundaries of the surface area of Class E airspace designated for an airport unless that person has prior authorization from Air Traffic Control (ATC). (PLT161) — 14 CFR §107.41

1080. According to 14 CFR part 107, how may a Remote Pilot in Command (Remote PIC) operate an unmanned aircraft in Class C airspace?

A— The Remote PIC must have prior authorization from the Air Traffic Control (ATC) facility having jurisdiction over that airspace.
B— The Remote PIC must contact the Air Traffic Control (ATC) facility after launching the unmanned aircraft.
C— The Remote PIC must monitor the Air Traffic Control (ATC) frequency from launch to recovery.

No person may operate a small unmanned aircraft in Class B, Class C, or Class D airspace or within the lateral boundaries of the surface area of Class E airspace designated for an airport unless that person has prior authorization from Air Traffic Control (ATC). (PLT161) — 14 CFR §107.41

1081. The lateral dimensions of Class D airspace are based on

A— the number of airports that lie within the Class D airspace.
B— 5 statute miles from the geographical center of the primary airport.
C— the instrument procedures for which the controlled airspace is established.

The dimensions of Class D airspace are as needed for each individual circumstance. The airspace may include extensions necessary for IFR arrival and departure paths. (PLT161) — AIM ¶3-2-5

1082. (Refer to Figure 74, area 6.) What airspace is Hayward Executive in?

A— Class B.
B— Class C.
C— Class D.

Hayward Executive is located in Class D airspace up to but not including 1,500 feet MSL as depicted by the blue segmented line surrounding it. Note that Class C begins at 1,500 feet MSL in that sector and goes up to the bottom of the overlying Class B (noted by the "T" in the altitude description). (PLT040) — AIM ¶3-2-5

1083. (Refer to Figure 26, area 5.) The airspace overlying and within 5 miles of Barnes County Airport is

A— Class D airspace from the surface to the floor of the overlying Class E airspace.
B— Class E airspace from the surface to 1,200 feet MSL.
C— Class G airspace from the surface up to but not including 700 feet AGL.

The Barnes County Airport is depicted inside the magenta shading, which is controlled airspace from 700 feet AGL up to but not including 18,000 feet. Therefore, the airspace below 700 feet AGL is Class G. (PLT040) — AIM ¶3-2-1

1084. (Refer to Figure 76.) What ATC permissions are required to operate near Anderson Airport?

A— ATC clearance required.
B— No ATC permission is required.
C— Waiver must be requested.

Refer to CT-8080-2X, Legend 1. Anderson Airport is in the bottom right quadrant of the sectional. The lack of shading around the airport indicates it is in Class G airspace. Small UAS operations in Class G airspace may be conducted without ATC permissions. However, remote pilots should exercise vigilance to ensure they cause no interruption to aircraft traffic. (PLT040) — Sectional Chart Legend

---

Answers

1079 [A]   1080 [A]   1081 [C]   1082 [C]   1083 [C]   1084 [B]

1085. (Refer to Figure 78.) In what airspace is Onawa, IA (K36) located?

A— Class E.
B— Class G.
C— Class D.

Onawa, IA (K36) is in the bottom right quadrant of the sectional excerpt. It is outside of any shading or lines, which indicates the airport is in Class G airspace up to 1,200 feet AGL. (PLT040) — Sectional Chart Legend

1284. What minimum radio equipment is required for operation within Class C airspace?

A— Two-way radio communications equipment and a 4096-code transponder.
B— Two-way radio communications equipment, a 4096-code transponder, and DME.
C— Two-way radio communications equipment, a 4096-code transponder, and an encoding altimeter.

Class C requires two-way radio communications equipment, a transponder, and an encoding altimeter. (PLT064) — FAA-H-8083-25

1301. What are the requirements for operating an sUAS in Class C airspace?

A— Two-way radio communications and transponder with altitude reporting capabilities.
B— Two-way radio communications and visual observer.
C— ATC authorization and visual observer.

Operations within Class C airspace require two-way radio communications, a transponder, and an encoding altimeter. (PLT064) — FAA-H-8083-25

1305. The typical outer radius limits of Class C airspace are

A— 10 NM.
B— 20 NM.
C— 30 NM.

The normal radius of the Class C outer area will be 20 NM. This is the area where separation is provided after two-way communication is established. It is only a requirement to contact ATC before entering the 10 NM Class C airspace depicted on the sectional chart. (PLT064) — FAA-H-8083-25

1307. (Refer to Figure 25, area 2.) The airspace directly overlying Addison Airport (ADS) is

A— Class D up to 3,000 feet MSL.
B— Class D up to but not including 3,000 feet MSL.
C— Class E from the surface up to 3,000 feet MSL.

Refer to Legend 1. Class D airspace is depicted with the dashed blue circle, the ceiling defined by the number in brackets [30]. (PLT064) — AIM ¶3-2-5

1295. (Refer to Figure 26, area 1.) The airspace overlying Tomlinson Airport is

A— Class G up to 18,000.
B— Class E from 1,200 up to but not including 18,000.
C— Class E from 700 up to but not including 18,000.

Refer to Legend 1. Tomlinson Airport is in the top left corner of Figure 26, and lies outside any colored circles. This indicates the airport is within Class E airspace from 1,200 feet AGL up to but not including 18,000 feet MSL. (PLT064) — AIM ¶3-2-5

1282. (Refer to Figure 78.) You have been hired to fly your UA to inspect train tracks from the town of Hinton to the town of Winnebago. Will you be able to conduct this flight without contacting ATC?

A— Yes, because you will remain under 400 feet.
B— No, because you will pass through Echo airspace.
C— No, because you will pass through Delta airspace.

Refer to Legend 1. The town of Hinton is north of Sioux City airport. Winnebago is south of Sioux City airport. This route is through the Class D airspace, depicted with the dashed blue line. You will need to contact ATC before conducting this flight. (PLT040) — Sectional Chart Legend

Answers

1085 [B]	1284 [C]	1301 [A]	1305 [B]	1307 [B]	1295 [B]
1282 [C]					

1086. (Refer to Figure 21.) You have been hired by a farmer to use your small unmanned aircraft to inspect his crops. The area that you are to survey is in the Devil's Lake West MOA, east of area 2. How would you find out if the MOA is active?

A— Refer to the legend for special use airspace phone number.
B— This information is available in the Small UAS database.
C— Refer to the Military Operations Directory.

A Military Operations Area (MOA) contains military training activities such as aerobatics, and calls for extreme caution. Any flight service station (FSS) within 100 miles of the area will provide information concerning MOA hours of operation. Prior to entering an active MOA, pilots should contact the controlling agency for traffic advisories, noted in the legend for special use airspace. (PLT376) — AIM ¶3-4-5

1087. Responsibility for collision avoidance in an alert area rests with

A— the controlling agency.
B— all pilots.
C— Air Traffic Control.

All activity within an Alert Area shall be conducted in accordance with FAA regulations, without waiver, and pilots of participating aircraft, as well as pilots transiting the area, shall be equally responsible for collision avoidance. (PLT376) — AIM ¶3-4-6

1088. (Refer to Figure 22, area 2.) At Coeur D'Alene, which frequency should be used as a Common Traffic Advisory Frequency (CTAF) to monitor airport traffic?

A— 122.05 MHz.
B— 135.075 MHz.
C— 122.8 MHz.

The Common Traffic Advisory Frequency (CTAF) is used for carrying out airport advisory practices and/or position reporting at an uncontrolled airport (which may also occur during hours when a tower is closed). The CTAF may be a UNICOM, MULTICOM, FSS, or tower frequency and is identified in the appropriate aeronautical publications. On charts, CTAF is indicated by a solid dot with the letter "C" inside. When the control tower operates part time and a UNICOM frequency is provided, use the UNICOM frequency. (PLT064) — AIM ¶4-1-9

1089. (Refer to Figure 26, area 4.) You have been hired to inspect the tower under construction at 46.9N and 98.6W, near Jamestown Regional (JMS). What must you receive prior to flying your unmanned aircraft in this area?

A— Authorization from the military.
B— Authorization from ATC.
C— Authorization from the National Park Service.

The magenta shading around Jamestown airport indicates the floor of the Class E airspace starts 700 feet above the surface. The dashed area means the Class E goes all the way to the surface. No person may operate a small unmanned aircraft in Class B, Class C, or Class D airspace or within the lateral boundaries of the surface area of Class E airspace designated for an airport unless that person has prior authorization from ATC. (PLT101) — 14 CFR §107.41, FAA-H-8083-25

1090. (Refer to Figure 59, area 2.) The chart shows a gray line with "VR1667, VR1617, VR1638, and VR1668." Could this area present a hazard to the operations of a small unmanned aircraft?

A— No, all operations will be above 400 feet.
B— Yes, this is a Military Training Route from 1,500 feet AGL and below.
C— Yes, the defined route provides traffic separation to manned aircraft.

VFR military training routes at and below 1,500 feet AGL (with no segment above 1,500) will be identified by four digit numbers, e.g., VR1351. VR above and below 1,500 feet AGL (segments of these routes may be below 1,500) will be identified by three digit numbers, e.g., VR426. Small UAS must operate below 400 feet. This 4-digit Military Training Route indicates operations below 1,500 feet AGL, which could present a hazard to the sUAS operation. (PLT064) — AIM ¶3-5-2

1091. (Refer to Figure 24, area 5.) You are operating an sUAS in the vicinity of Sulphur Springs Airport (SUR) where there is active air traffic. Who has priority and right-of-way within the traffic pattern area?

A— Priority and right-of-way goes to the aircraft closest to the landing runway.
B— The sUAS.
C— The existing manned aircraft.

No person may operate a small unmanned aircraft in a manner that interferes with operations and traffic patterns at any airport, heliport, or seaplane base. (PLT414) — 14 CFR §107.43

Answers

1086 [A]   1087 [B]   1088 [C]   1089 [B]   1090 [B]   1091 [C]

1296. Where can you find information about operating in an MOA along your planned route of flight?

A— Sectional chart.
B— Chart supplement.
C— Aeronautical Information Manual.

Refer to Legend 1. Military Operations Areas (MOA) are depicted on sectional charts with a shaded, hashed magenta line. You can find information about the MOA on the back of the sectional, including times of operation, altitudes affected, and the controlling agency. (PLT040) — AIM ¶3-4-5

1092. (Refer to Figure 71, area 6.) Sky Way Airport is

A— an airport restricted to use by private and recreational pilots.
B— a restricted military stage field within restricted airspace.
C— a nonpublic use airport.

The "Pvt" after the airport name indicates Sky Way Airport is a restricted or non-public use airport. (PLT064) — Sectional Chart

Answer (A) is incorrect because the R in the circle indicates the airport is a nonpublic use airport. Answer (B) is incorrect because the blue box near Sky Way Airport indicates an alert area.

1093. (Refer to Figure 71, area 1.) The floor of the Class E airspace above Georgetown Airport (E36) is at

A— the surface.
B— 700 feet AGL.
C— 3,823 feet MSL.

Georgetown Airport is outside the magenta shaded area, which indicates the floor of Class E airspace is at 1,200 feet AGL. The airport elevation is given in the airport data as 2,623 feet MSL. Therefore, the Class E airspace above Georgetown Airport is 3,823 feet MSL (2,623 + 1,200). (PLT040) — Sectional Chart

Answer (A) is incorrect because Class E airspace begins at the surface only when surrounded by a magenta segmented circle. Answer (B) is incorrect because Class E airspace begins at 700 feet AGL inside the magenta shaded areas.

1094. (Refer to Figure 75.) The airspace surrounding the Gila Bend AF AUX Airport (GXF) (area 6) is classified as Class

A— B.
B— C.
C— D.

The GXF airport is surrounded by a dashed blue line which indicates it is within Class D airspace. (PLT040) — Sectional Chart

1095. Under what condition, if any, may remote pilots fly through a restricted area?

A— When flying on airways with an ATC clearance.
B— With the controlling agency's authorization.
C— Regulations do not allow this.

Restricted areas can be penetrated but only with the permission of the controlling agency. No person may operate an aircraft within a restricted area contrary to the restrictions imposed unless he/she has the permission of the using or controlling agency. Penetration of restricted areas without authorization from the using or controlling agency may be fatal to the aircraft and its occupants. (PLT376) — 14 CFR §107.45, AIM ¶3-4-3

1309. (Refer to Figure 75, area 6.) Where can you find additional information about "R-2305"?

A— On the Special Use Airspace section of the chart.
B— In the Aeronautical Information Manual.
C— In the Chart Supplements U.S. (Formerly A/FD).

Refer to Legend 1. Restricted areas are identified on sectional charts with an "R" followed by a number. You can find information about restricted areas on the back of the sectional chart. (PLT040) — FAA-H-8083-25

Answers

1296 [A]	1092 [C]	1093 [C]	1094 [C]	1095 [B]	1309 [A]

Topography

To identify a point on the surface of the earth, a geographic coordinate, or "grid" system was devised. By reference to meridians of longitude and parallels of latitude, any position may be accurately located when using the grid system.

Equidistant from the poles is an imaginary circle called the equator. The lines running east and west, parallel to the equator are called parallels of latitude, and are used to measure angular distance north or south of the equator. From the equator to either pole is 90°, with 0° being at the equator, while 90° north latitude describes the location of the North Pole. *See* Figure 2-2. Lines called meridians of longitude are drawn from pole to pole at right angles to the equator. The prime meridian, used as the zero degree line, passes through Greenwich, England. From this line, measurements are made in degrees both easterly and westerly up to 180°.

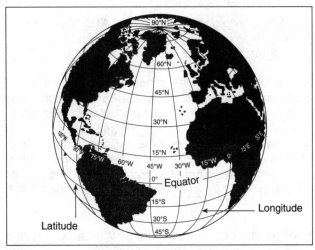

Figure 2-2. Meridians of longitude and parallels of latitude

Any specific geographical point can be located by reference to its longitude and latitude. For example, Washington, DC is approximately 39° north of the equator and 77° west of the prime meridian and would be stated as 39°N 77°W. Note that latitude is stated first.

A Sectional Chart is a pictorial representation of a portion of the Earth's surface upon which lines and symbols in a variety of colors represent features and/or details that can be seen on the Earth's surface. Contour lines, shaded relief, color tints, obstruction symbols, and maximum elevation figures are all used to show topographical information. Explanations and examples may be found in the chart legend. Remote pilots should become familiar with all of the information provided in each Sectional Chart Legend, found in Legend 1 in the CT-8080-2X.

In order to describe a location more precisely, each degree (°) is subdivided into 60 minutes (') and each minute further divided into 60 seconds ("), although seconds are not shown. Thus, the location of the airport at Elk City, Oklahoma is described as being at 35°25'55"N 99°23'15"W (35 degrees, 25 minutes, 55 seconds north latitude; 99 degrees, 23 minutes, 15 seconds west longitude). Degrees of west longitude increase moving west from the prime meridian until reaching the international line and degrees of east longitude increase moving east from the prime meridian to the international date line. Degrees of north latitude increase moving north from the equator to the north pole and degrees of south latitude increase moving south from the equator to the south pole.

1096. (Refer to Figure 26.) What does the line of latitude at area 4 measure?

A— The degrees of latitude east and west of the Prime Meridian.

B— The degrees of latitude north and south of the equator.

C— The degrees of latitude east and west of the line that passes through Greenwich, England.

The "47" at area 4 is the line of latitude (also referred to as a parallel) north and south of the equator. (PLT064) — FAA-H-8083-25

Answers

1096 [B]

1097. (Refer to Figure 69.) What does the line of longitude at area 7 measure?

A— The degrees of longitude north and south of the prime meridian.

B— The degrees of longitude north and south from the equator.

C— The degrees of longitude east and west of the line that passes through Greenwich, England.

The "98" north of area 7 is the line of longitude (also referred to as meridian) east and west of the prime meridian which passes through Greenwich, England. (PLT064) — FAA-H-8083-25

1098. Which statement about longitude and latitude is true?

A— Lines of longitude are parallel to the Equator.

B— Lines of longitude cross the Equator at right angles.

C— The 0° line of latitude passes through Greenwich, England.

Meridians of longitude encircle the earth from pole to pole, and all meridians cross the equator at right angles. (PLT064) — FAA-H-8083-25

Answer (A) is incorrect because lines of latitude are parallel to the equator. Answer (C) is incorrect because the 0° line of longitude passes through Greenwich, England.

1099. (Refer to Figure 21.) What airport is located approximately 47 (degrees) 40 (minutes) N latitude and 101 (degrees) 26 (minutes) W longitude?

A— Mercer County Regional Airport.

B— Semshenko Airport.

C— Garrison Airport.

Graticules on Sectional Charts are the lines dividing each 30 minutes of latitude and each 30 minutes of longitude. Each tick mark represents one minute of latitude or longitude. Latitude increases northward, west longitude increases going westward. The Garrison (Pvt) Airport is located at approximately 47°40"N latitude and 101°26'00"W longitude. (PLT064) — FAA-H-8083-25

1100. (Refer to Figure 20, area 3.) With ATC authorization, you are operating your small unmanned aircraft approximately 4 SM southeast of Elizabeth City Regional Airport (ECG). What hazard is indicated to be in that area?

A— High density military operations in the vicinity.

B— Unmarked balloon on a cable up to 3,008 feet AGL.

C— Unmarked balloon on a cable up to 3,008 feet MSL.

The sectional chart excerpt includes a blue box note 4 SM southeast of the ECG airport that says "Caution: Unmarked balloon on cable to 3008' MSL. Check NOTAMs." (PLT064) — Sectional Chart Legend

1101. (Refer to Figure 20, area 2.) Why would the small flag at Lake Drummond be important to a remote pilot?

A— This is a VFR check point for manned aircraft, and a higher volume of air traffic should be expected there.

B— This is a GPS check point that can be used by both manned and remote pilots for orientation.

C— This indicates that there will be a large obstruction depicted on the next printing of the chart.

Refer to Legend 1. The flag symbol represents a visual checkpoint used by manned aircraft to identify the position to initiate their contact with Norfolk Approach Control. As a defined checkpoint, a higher volume of air traffic should be expected there. (PLT064) — Sectional Chart Legend, FAA-H-8083-25

1102. Which is true concerning the blue and magenta colors used to depict airports on Sectional Aeronautical Charts?

A— Airports with control towers underlying Class A, B, and C airspace are shown in blue, Class D and E airspace are magenta.

B— Airports with control towers underlying Class C, D, and E airspace are shown in magenta.

C— Airports with control towers underlying Class B, C, D, and E airspace are shown in blue.

Refer to Legend 1. Airports having control towers are shown in blue, all others in magenta. (PLT064) — Sectional Chart Legend

Answer (A) is incorrect because Class A airspace is not depicted on a sectional chart; Class C airspace is magenta; and Class E airspace is both blue and magenta depending on where the floor of the airspace starts. Answer (B) is incorrect because airports with control towers are shown in blue.

1103. (Refer to Figure 23, area 3.) What is the height of the lighted obstacle approximately 6 nautical miles southwest of Savannah International?

A— 1,500 feet MSL.
B— 1,531 feet AGL.
C— 1,548 feet MSL.

Refer to Legend 1. The top number, printed in bold, is the height of the obstruction above mean sea level. The second number, printed in parentheses, is the height of the obstruction above ground level. The obstruction is shown as 1,548 feet MSL and 1,534 feet AGL. (PLT064) — Sectional Chart Legend

1104. (Refer to Figure 23, area 3.) The top of the group obstruction approximately 11 nautical miles from the Savannah VORTAC on the 009° radial is

A— 400 feet AGL.
B— 454 feet MSL.
C— 432 feet MSL.

Refer to Legend 1. On Figure 23, area 3, the group obstruction near the 009° radial has the word "stacks" below 454. The bold number (454) indicates the height of the obstruction above mean sea level. (PLT064) — Sectional Chart Legend

1105. (Refer to Figure 24, area 2.) Operating an sUAS, can you vertically clear the obstacle on the southeast side of Winnsboro Airport?

A— Yes.
B— No.
C— Maybe.

The elevation of the top of the obstacle is shown as 903 feet above mean sea level (MSL). Small UAS operations may not exceed 400 feet AGL. Moreover, the sUAS may be operated higher than 400 feet AGL if the sUAS is flown within a 400 foot radius of the structure and does not fly higher than 400 feet above the structure's immediate uppermost limit. (PLT064) — Sectional Chart Legend, 14 CFR §107.51

1106. (Refer to Figure 26, area 1.) You have been asked to inspect the tower just north of Binford. What restrictions should the remote PIC be concerned with prior to operating the sUAS?

A— None, the tower is in Class G airspace up to 1,200 AGL.
B— Class E airspace begins at the ground as indicated by the blue hashed lines surrounding the area.
C— Restricted airspace exists around the tower thus permission is required from the controlling agency.

No person may operate a small unmanned aircraft in prohibited or restricted areas unless that person has permission from the using or controlling agency, as appropriate. (PLT064) — Sectional Chart Legend, 14 CFR §107.45

1107. (Refer to Figure 24, area 1.) How close can the Remote PIC fly their sUAS to the Majors airport (GVT) without having to contact ATC?

A— 4 Nautical Miles (NM)
B— 4 Statute Miles (SM)
C— Remote PICs must contact ATC whenever operating within the magenta shading on Sectional Charts.

Contact with ATC must be made when operating within Class D airport, which is indicated by the blue airport and the blue dashed line surrounding it. The radius of Class D in the case is 4 NM, which is the common standard radius, although configuration of Class D is individually tailored for some airports. (PLT064) — Sectional Chart Legend, 14 CFR §107.41, AIM ¶3-2-5

Answers

1103 [C]   1104 [B]   1105 [A]   1106 [C]   1107 [A]

1108. (Refer to Figure 22, area 1.) You have been contracted to photograph Lake Pend Oreille from a vantage point just east of Cocolalla. You notice there is a hill which should provide a good place to take panoramic photographs. What is the maximum altitude (MSL) you are authorized to fly over the hill?

A— You cannot operate your sUAS above 400 MSL, and thus cannot operate anywhere in this part of the country.

B— You may operate up to 5,360 feet MSL in Class G airspace.

C— You cannot operate your sUAS without ATC permission because you will be in Class E airspace above 1,200 MSL.

The hill has a height of 4,960 MSL; therefore an sUAS may be flown up to 400 feet AGL, which is 5,360 feet. The floor of airspace such as Class E is in AGL not MSL. (PLT064) — Sectional Chart Legend, 14 CFR §107.51

1109. (Refer to Figure 20, area 3.) What is the latitude and longitude location of the Elizabeth City CGAS RGL (ECG)?

A— N 36° 16' W 76° 10'

B— W 36° 16' N 76° 10'

C— N 37° 0' W 77° 10'

To measure the latitude and longitude, begin with looking for the hatched black lines with degree numbers on them. Just southeast of ECG there is the 36° latitude line (running east/west) and the 76° longitude line (running north/south). Count the ticks on the latitude line which is approximately 16—these are the number of minutes yielding N 36° 16' (north because the airport is north of the equator). Next, count the ticks west of the longitude line. There are approximately 10, therefore this is W 76° 10' (west because the airport is west of the prime meridian). (PLT064) — Sectional Chart Legend

1110. (Refer to Figure 20, area 3.) You need to operate your sUAS in close proximity of the Elizabeth City CGAS RGL (ECG) airport. What frequency should be used to contact ATC?

A— 122.95

B— 124.375

C— 120.50

According to the chart, the ATC control tower frequency is 120.50. (PLT064) — Sectional Chart Legend

Airport Operations

When operating in the vicinity of an airport, the remote PIC must be aware of all traffic patterns and approach corridors to runways and landing areas. Sources for this airport data include the Sectional Chart and the *Chart Supplement U.S.* The remote PIC must avoid operating anywhere that the presence of the sUAS may interfere with airport operations, such as approach corridors, taxiways, runways, or helipads. Furthermore, the remote PIC must yield right-of-way to all other aircraft, including aircraft operating on the surface of the airport.

Remote PICs are prohibited from operating their small UA in a manner that interferes with operations and traffic patterns at airports, heliports, and seaplane bases. While a small UA must always yield right-of-way to a manned aircraft, a manned aircraft may alter its flightpath, delay its landing, or take off in order to avoid an sUAS that may present a potential conflict or otherwise affect the safe outcome of the flight. For example, a UA hovering 200 feet above a runway may cause a manned aircraft holding short of the runway to delay takeoff, or a manned aircraft on the downwind leg of the pattern to delay landing. While the UA in this scenario would not pose an immediate traffic conflict to the aircraft on the downwind leg of the traffic pattern or to the aircraft intending to take off, nor would it violate the right-of-way rules, the small UA would nevertheless have interfered with the operations of the traffic pattern at an airport.

ATC towers are established to promote the safe, orderly, and expeditious flow of air traffic. The tower controller will issue instructions for aircraft to follow the desired flight path while in the airport traffic area whenever necessary by using terminology as shown in Figure 2-3. Manned aircraft use this

Continued

Answers

1108 [B]   1109 [A]   1110 [C]

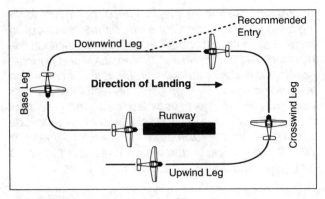

Figure 2-3. Manned aircraft traffic pattern.

same terminology to self-announce position and intentions, consistent with recommended traffic advisory procedures.

In order to avoid interfering with operations in a traffic pattern, remote PICs should avoid operating in the traffic pattern or published approach corridors used by manned aircraft. When operational necessity requires the remote PIC to operate at an airport in uncontrolled airspace, the remote PIC should operate the small UA in such a way that the manned aircraft pilot does not need to alter his or her flightpath in the traffic pattern or on a published instrument approach in order to avoid a potential collision. Because remote PICs have an obligation to yield right-of-way to all other aircraft and avoid interfering in traffic pattern operations, the FAA expects that most remote PICs will avoid operating in the vicinity of airports because their aircraft generally do not require airport infrastructure, and the concentration of other aircraft increases in the vicinity of airports.

The FAA has the authority to approve or deny aircraft operations based on traffic density, controller workload, communication issues, or any other type of operations that could potentially impact the safe and expeditious flow of air traffic in that airspace. Those planning sUAS operations in controlled airspace are encouraged to contact the FAA as early as possible.

When ATC authorization is required (at or near an airport with a control tower and/or when operating within controlled airspace), it must be requested and granted before any operation in that airspace. The time required for approval will vary based on the resources available at the ATC facility and the complexity and safety issues raised by each specific request. For this reason, remote PICs should contact the appropriate ATC facility as soon as possible prior to any operation in Class B, C and D airspace and within the lateral boundaries of the surface area of Class E airspace designated for an airport.

When ATC authorization is not required (at or near an airport without a control tower and/or when operating within uncontrolled airspace), remote pilots should monitor the CTAF to stay aware of manned aircraft communications and operations. For the sake of safety, it is advisable for remote PICs to announce their sUAS activity on the CTAF to make manned pilots aware of such operations.

For recurring or long-term operations in a given location, prior authorization could include a **letter of agreement (LOA)**, established with the controlling ATC facility for that airspace, to establish sUAS operating procedures. This LOA will outline the ability to integrate into the existing air traffic operation and may improve the likelihood of access to the airspace where operations are proposed. This agreement will ensure all parties involved are aware of limitations and conditions and will enable the safe flow of aircraft operations in that airspace. For short-term or short-notice operations proposed in controlled airport airspace, a LOA may not be feasible. Prior authorization is required in all cases.

All areas on-airport that are used for certain cargo and passenger functions, including screening, must be a **security identification display area (SIDA)**. A SIDA is that portion of an airport within the United States, specified in the security program, in which individuals must display an airport-issued or approved identification and carry out other security measures.

Answers

1111. (Refer to Figure 80.) What do the blue shaded lines indicate throughout this sectional excerpt?

A— Military training routes.
B— Airline corridors.
C— Victor airways.

Refer to Legend 1. The routes established between VORs are depicted by blue-tinted bands showing the airway number following the letter "V," and are called "Victor airways." Remote pilots should exercise vigilance in looking for other aircraft when operating near these high density areas. (PLT064) — Sectional Chart Legend

1112. The recommended entry position for manned aircraft to enter an airport traffic pattern is

A— 45° to the base leg just below traffic pattern altitude.
B— to enter 45° at the midpoint of the downwind leg at traffic pattern altitude.
C— to cross directly over the airport at traffic pattern altitude and join the downwind leg.

The recommended entry position for an airport traffic pattern is 45° to the midpoint of the downwind leg at traffic pattern altitude. (PLT146) — AIM ¶4-3-3

1113. When a manned aircraft is approaching to land at an airport in Class G airspace without an operating control tower, the pilot will

A— enter and fly a traffic pattern at 800 feet AGL.
B— make all turns to the left, unless otherwise indicated.
C— fly a left-hand traffic pattern at 800 feet AGL.

When a manned aircraft is approaching to land at an airport in Class G airspace without an operating control tower, each pilot of an airplane will make all turns to the left unless the airport displays approved light signals or visual markings indicating that turns should be made to the right (which will be detailed in the Chart Supplement U.S. (PLT146) — 14 CFR §91.126

Answers (A) and (C) are incorrect because the traffic pattern altitude will vary for each airport and aircraft; however, all turns should be to the left unless otherwise indicated.

1114. Entries into traffic patterns by manned aircraft while descending create specific collision hazards and

A— should be avoided.
B— should be used whenever possible.
C— are illegal.

Entries into traffic patterns while descending create specific collision hazards and should be avoided. (PLT146) — AIM ¶4-4-15

1115. What is required to enter an airport SIDA?

A— You must pass the TSA screening.
B— You must have an FAA-issued pilot certificate.
C— You must have an airport-issued or approved ID.

On-airport areas that are used for certain cargo functions, including screening, must be a security identification display area (SIDA). A SIDA is that portion of an airport within the United States, specified in the security program, in which individuals must display an airport-issued or approved ID and carry out other security measures. (PLT498) — 49 CFR §1544

Airport Markings and Signs

Remote pilots need to be familiar with standard airport markings and signs to exercise vigilant collision avoidance, practice sound see-and-avoid procedures, and not interfere with manned aircraft operations.

Runway numbers and letters are determined from the approach direction. The number is the magnetic heading of the runway rounded to the nearest 10°. For example, a runway facing an azimuth of 183° would result in a runway number of 18; a runway with a magnetic azimuth of 076° would result in a runway numbered 8. If there is more than one runway facing the same direction, the runway will have letters to differentiate between left (L), right (R), or center (C). *See* Figure 2-4.

The designated beginning of the runway that is available and suitable for the landing of aircraft is called the threshold (Figure 2-5a). A threshold that is not at the beginning of the full-strength runway pavement is a displaced threshold. The paved area behind the displaced threshold is marked by arrows

Continued

Answers
1111 [C]   1112 [B]   1113 [B]   1114 [A]   1115 [C]

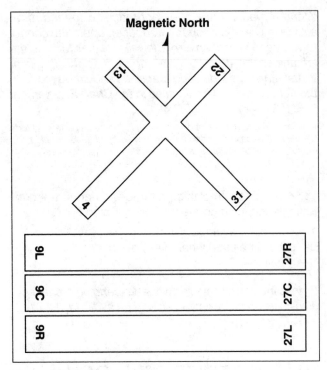

Figure 2-4. Runway numbers and letters

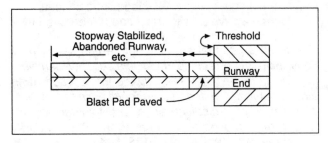

Figure 2-6. Stopway marking

(Figure 2-5b) and is available for taxiing, take-off, and landing rollout, but is not to be used for landing, usually because of an obstruction in the approach path. *See* Figure 2-5.

Stopways are found extending beyond some usable runways. These areas are marked by chevrons, and while they appear usable, they are suitable only as overrun areas. *See* Figure 2-6.

A closed runway which is unusable for various reasons and may be hazardous, even though it may appear usable, will be marked by an "X."

A basic runway may only have centerline markings and runway numbers. Airports supporting instrument operations, higher volumes, and larger aircraft may use additional runway markings. *See* Figure 2-7.

Aircraft use taxiways to transition from parking areas to the runway. Taxiways are identified by a continuous yellow centerline stripe and may include edge markings to define the edge of the taxiway. Where a taxiway approaches a runway, there may be a holding position marker. These consist of four yellow lines (two solid and two dashed). The solid lines are where the aircraft is to hold. Beyond this point, an aircraft is considered to be on the runway.

There are six types of signs that may be found at airports. *See* Figure 2-8. The more complex the layout of an airport, the more important the signs become to pilots. The six types of signs are:

• Mandatory instruction signs—red background with white inscription. These signs denote an entrance to a runway, critical area, or prohibited area.

• Location signs—black with yellow inscription and a yellow border, no arrows. They are used to identify a taxiway or runway location, to identify the boundary of the runway, or identify an instrument landing system (ILS) critical area.

Continued

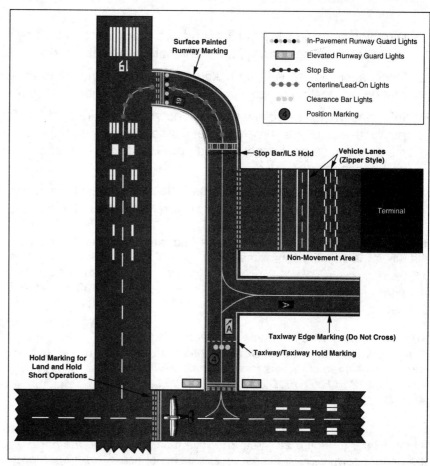

Figure 2-7. Selected airport markings and surface lighting

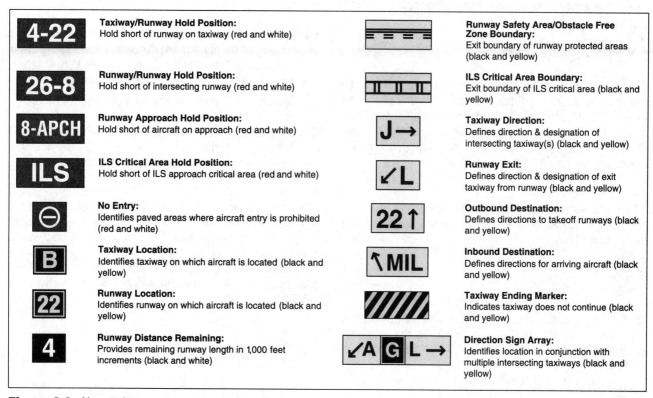

Taxiway/Runway Hold Position:
Hold short of runway on taxiway (red and white)

Runway/Runway Hold Position:
Hold short of intersecting runway (red and white)

Runway Approach Hold Position:
Hold short of aircraft on approach (red and white)

ILS Critical Area Hold Position:
Hold short of ILS approach critical area (red and white)

No Entry:
Identifies paved areas where aircraft entry is prohibited
(red and white)

Taxiway Location:
Identifies taxiway on which aircraft is located (black and
yellow)

Runway Location:
Identifies runway on which aircraft is located (black and
yellow)

Runway Distance Remaining:
Provides remaining runway length in 1,000 feet
increments (black and white)

**Runway Safety Area/Obstacle Free
Zone Boundary:**
Exit boundary of runway protected areas
(black and yellow)

ILS Critical Area Boundary:
Exit boundary of ILS critical area (black and
yellow)

Taxiway Direction:
Defines direction & designation of
intersecting taxiway(s) (black and yellow)

Runway Exit:
Defines direction & designation of exit
taxiway from runway (black and yellow)

Outbound Destination:
Defines directions to takeoff runways (black
and yellow)

Inbound Destination:
Defines directions for arriving aircraft (black
and yellow)

Taxiway Ending Marker:
Indicates taxiway does not continue (black
and yellow)

Direction Sign Array:
Identifies location in conjunction with
multiple intersecting taxiways (black and
yellow)

Figure 2-8. Airport signs

- Direction signs—yellow background with black inscription. The inscription identifies the designation of the intersecting taxiway(s) leading out of an intersection.
- Destination signs—yellow background with black inscription and arrows. These signs provide information on locating areas, such as runways, terminals, cargo areas, and civil aviation areas.
- Information signs—yellow background with black inscription. These signs are used to provide the pilot with information on areas that cannot be seen from the control tower, applicable radio frequencies, and noise abatement procedures. The airport operator determines the need, size, and location of these signs.
- Runway distance remaining signs—black background with white numbers. The numbers indicate the distance of the remaining runway in thousands of feet.

1116. The numbers 9 and 27 on a runway indicate that the runway is oriented approximately

A— 009° and 027° true.
B— 090° and 270° true.
C— 090° and 270° magnetic.

The runway number is the whole number nearest one-tenth the magnetic azimuth of the centerline of the runway, measured clockwise from magnetic north. For example: 272° = RWY 27; 087° = RWY 9. (PLT141) — AIM ¶2-3-3

1117. (Refer to Figure 26, area 2.) While monitoring the Cooperstown CTAF you hear an aircraft announce that they are midfield left downwind to RWY 13. Where would the aircraft be relative to the runway?

A— The aircraft is East.
B— The aircraft is South.
C— The aircraft is West.

Cooperstown Airport depicts one runway; RWY 13 means the aircraft will be headed 130 degrees upon landing. "Left downwind" means the aircraft is currently to the left side, heading opposite and midway of the landing runway. This would place the aircraft east of the landing runway. (PLT146) — AIM ¶4-1-5

1118. An aircraft announces that they are on short final for runway 9. Where will the aircraft be in relation to the airport?

A— North
B— West
C— East

On final approach to runway 9, the aircraft will be heading from west to east on a 090 heading. Thus the aircraft is west of the airport. (PLT146) — AIM ¶4-1-5

1119. You are conducting sUAS operations northeast of a nearby airport. While monitoring the CTAF, an aircraft announces that it is departing runway 36 utilizing a right traffic pattern. Will the aircraft potentially conflict with your operation?

A— No, the aircraft will be flying on the west side of the airport.
B— No, the aircraft will be flying to the south of the airport.
C— Yes, the aircraft may overfly northeast of the airport.

If taking off of runway 36, the aircraft will be departing to the north on a 360 heading. With right traffic, it will turn right towards the northeast on the crosswind leg. (PLT146) — AIM ¶4-1-5

1120. While operating a sUAS just south of a controlled airport with authorization, ATC notifies you to stay clear of the runway 6 final approach course. What action should you take to comply with this request?

A— Stay clear of areas to the west and north of your area of operation.
B— Stay clear of areas to the east and north of your area of operation.
C— Stay clear of areas to the west and south of your area of operation.

Runway 6 faces northeast on a 060 heading thus arriving aircraft will be on final approach southwest of the airport. Since you are operating south of the airport, you would want to avoid areas west (which would be closer to the final approach course) and north (closer to the airport and possibly the final approach course for runway 6). (PLT146) — AIM ¶4-1-5

Answers

1116 [C]   1117 [A]   1118 [B]   1119 [C]   1120 [A]

1121. When turning onto a taxiway from another taxiway, what is the purpose of the taxiway directional sign?

A— Indicates direction to take-off runway.
B— Indicates designation and direction of exit taxiway from runway.
C— Indicates designation and direction of taxiway leading out of an intersection.

The taxiway directional sign identifies the designation(s) of the intersecting taxiway(s) leading out of the intersection that a pilot would normally be expected to turn onto or hold short of. (PLT141) — AIM ¶2-3-10

Answer (A) is incorrect because this is the purpose of the runway location sign. Answer (B) is incorrect because this is the purpose of the destination sign.

1122. When approaching holding lines from the side with the continuous lines, the pilot

A— may continue taxiing.
B— should not cross the lines without ATC clearance.
C— should continue taxiing until all parts of the aircraft have crossed the lines.

When approaching the holding line from the side with the continuous lines, a pilot should not cross the holding line without ATC clearance at a controlled airport, or without making sure of adequate separation from other aircraft at uncontrolled airports. (PLT141) — AIM ¶2-3-5

Answers (A) and (C) are incorrect because no part of the aircraft may cross the hold line without ATC clearance.

1123. What is the purpose of the runway/runway hold position sign?

A— Denotes entrance to runway from a taxiway.
B— Denotes area protected for an aircraft approaching or departing a runway.
C— Denotes intersecting runways.

Mandatory instruction signs are used to denote an entrance to a runway or critical area and areas where an aircraft is prohibited from entering. The runway holding position sign is located at the holding position on taxiways that intersect a runway or on runways that intersect other runways. (PLT141) — AIM ¶2-3-8

1124. What is the purpose for the runway hold position markings on the taxiway?

A— Holds aircraft short of the runway.
B— Allows an aircraft permission onto the runway.
C— Identifies area where aircraft are prohibited.

Runway holding position markings on taxiways identify the locations on a taxiway where an aircraft is supposed to stop when it does not have clearance to proceed onto the runway. (PLT141) — AIM ¶2-3-5

1125. Holding position signs have

A— red inscriptions on white background.
B— white inscriptions on red background.
C— yellow inscriptions on red background.

Hold position signs have white inscriptions on red background. (PLT141) — AIM ¶2-3-5

Answers (A) and (C) are incorrect because these color combination are not used in airport signs.

1126. What is the purpose of the No Entry sign?

A— Identifies a paved area where aircraft are prohibited from entering.
B— Identifies area that does not continue beyond intersection.
C— Identifies the exit boundary for the runway protected area.

The no entry sign prohibits an aircraft from entering an area. Typically, this sign would be located on a taxiway intended to be used in only one direction or at the intersection of vehicle roadways with runways, taxiways or aprons where the roadway may be mistaken as a taxiway or other aircraft movement surface. (PLT141) — AIM ¶2-3-8

Answer (B) is incorrect because this is the purpose of a hold position sign. Answer (C) is incorrect because this is the purpose of the runway boundary sign.

1127. The "taxiway ending" marker

A— indicates taxiway does not continue.
B— identifies area where aircraft are prohibited.
C— provides general taxiing direction to named taxiway.

Taxiway ending markers are used to indicate that the taxiway does not continue. (PLT141) — AIM ¶2-3-4

Answers

1121 [C]	1122 [B]	1123 [C]	1124 [A]	1125 [B]	1126 [A]
1127 [A]					

1128. Which publication contains an explanation of airport signs and markings?

A— Aeronautical Information Manual (AIM).
B— Advisory Circulars (AC).
C— Chart Supplement U.S.

Both the Aeronautical Information Manual (AIM) and the Pilot's Handbook of Aeronautical Knowledge (FAA-H-8083-25) contain explanations of airport signs and markings. (PLT116) — AIM Chapter 2, Section 3

Answer (B) is incorrect because ACs provide information on non-regulatory material of interest. Answer (C) is incorrect because the Chart Supplement U.S. provides only comprehensive information on a given airport (such as runway lengths, available services, lighting, etc.).

1129. You have received authorization to operate an sUAS at an airport. When flying the sUAS, the ATC tower instructs you to stay clear of all runways. Which situation would indicate that you are complying with this request?

A— You are on the double dashed yellow line side of markings near the runway.
B— You are over dashed white lines in the center of the pavement.
C— You are on the double solid yellow line side of markings near the runway.

Runway hold markings are indicated by two dashed and two solid yellow lines. You are considered to be on the taxiway on the double solid yellow line side while you are considered to be on the runway if on the double dashed yellow line side. (PLT141) — AIM ¶2-3-4

Answer (A) is incorrect because the double dashed yellow line would indicate you are on the taxiway. Answer (B) is incorrect because the dashed white centerline markings would indicate that you are on the runway.

Collision Avoidance

A key component to avoiding both manned and unmanned aircraft is active collision avoidance procedures. Scanning the sky for other aircraft is a critical factor in collision avoidance. Remote pilots and visual observers must develop an effective scanning technique that maximizes visual capabilities. Because the eyes focus only on a narrow viewing area, effective scanning is accomplished with a series of short, regularly spaced eye movements. Each movement should not exceed 10°, and each area should be observed for at least one second. Any aircraft that appears to have no relative motion and stays in one scan quadrant is likely to be on a collision course. If a target shows neither lateral nor vertical motion, but increases in size, take evasive action.

Another critical component to collision avoidance is avoiding operations near and under moored balloons and helicopters. The helicopter community performs their critical operations typically at 1,000 feet or less and often in a wire/obstruction rich environment. It is important to note that not all wires are marked.

Inflight Hazards

Although most sUAS cannot be operated in precipitation or other adverse weather conditions, remote PICs should be aware that static electricity buildup (sometimes referred to as P-static) can occur when an aircraft in flight comes in contact with rain, snow, fog, sleet, hail, volcanic ash, dust; any solid or liquid particles. In a very short period of time a substantial negative charge will develop on the skin of the aircraft. If the aircraft is not equipped with static dischargers, or has an ineffective static discharger system, when a sufficient negative voltage level is reached the aircraft may develop a phenomenon called a "corona," a luminous manifestation of the static electricity accumulation. Such buildups may discharge from the extremities of the aircraft, such as the wing tips, horizontal stabilizer, vertical stabilizer, antenna, propeller tips, etc. The visible discharge of static electricity is referred to as "St. Elmo's fire." P-static can also disrupt communications between the sUAS and the control station which may have significant detrimental impact on the ability to control or retrieve the sUAS. Some sUAS may use static dischargers to address this problem.

Answers

1128 [A]   1129 [C]

In recent years, the use of lasers has had more of an impact on all types of flight operations. Of concern to NAS users are those laser events that may affect pilots, e.g., outdoor laser light shows or demonstrations for entertainment and advertisements at special events and theme parks. Generally, the beams from these events appear as bright blue-green in color; however, they may be red, yellow, or white, and some laser systems produce light that is invisible to the human eye. FAA regulations prohibit the disruption of aviation activity by any person on the ground or in the air.

Remote pilots should be aware that illumination from these laser operations are able to create temporary vision impairment miles from the actual location. In addition, these operations can cause permanent eye damage. Remote pilots should therefore use caution when using sUAS in and around known laser activity. Extreme caution should be exercised if an sUAS is fitted with a laser as it could potentially cause hazards to manned aircraft, the public, or even the remote PIC or other crewmembers. Pilots should make themselves aware of where these activities are being conducted and avoid these areas if possible. When these activities become known to the FAA, NOTAMs are issued to inform the aviation community of the events. Pilots should consult NOTAMs or the Special Notices section of the *Chart Supplement U.S.* for information regarding these activities.

Although remote pilots should typically avoid operations in and around power plants, industrial production facilities, or other industrial systems, there may be times when such activity is sanctioned by the owners of these facilities for inspection or imaging. These types of locations often have thermal plumes, which are visible or invisible emissions of large amounts of vertically directed unstable gases. High temperature exhaust plumes may cause significant air disturbances such as turbulence and vertical shear. Other identified potential hazards include, but are not necessarily limited to, reduced visibility, oxygen depletion, engine particulate contamination, exposure to gaseous oxides, and/or icing. Results of encountering a plume may include airframe damage, aircraft upset, and/or engine damage/failure. These conditions could quickly lead to damage and/or loss of control of an sUAS. These hazards are most critical during low altitude flight, especially during maneuvering, takeoff and landing. When able, a pilot should fly upwind of possible thermal plumes. When a plume is visible via smoke or a condensation cloud, remain clear yet at the same time, realize that a plume may have both visible and invisible characteristics. Remote pilots are encouraged to exercise caution when operating in the vicinity of thermal plumes. Refer to the *Chart Supplement U.S.* where the airports' amplifying notes may warn pilots and identify the location of structure(s) emitting thermal plumes.

Most skeletal structures are supported by guy wires, which are very difficult to see in good weather and can be invisible at dusk or during periods of reduced visibility. These wires can extend about 1,500 feet horizontally from a structure; therefore, all skeletal structures should be avoided horizontally by at least 2,000 feet.

Birds and wildlife pose a particular threat to aircraft operations. Although catastrophic events are rare in manned aviation, sUAS are particularly vulnerable to such events. Collision with wildlife will likely cause significant damage and/or loss of control. Remote pilots should report collisions between aircraft and wildlife to assist in the tracking of these incidents and to potentially take action to mitigate future risks of these events. Reports may be sent to the FAA via their Wildlife Strike Report system (**http://wildlife.faa.gov/strikenew.aspx**). Many airports advise pilots of other wildlife hazards through the *Chart Supplement U.S.* and the NOTAM system.

Collisions between aircraft and animals have been increasing and are not limited to rural airports, as these accidents have also occurred at several major airports. Pilots should exercise extreme caution when warned of the presence of wildlife on and in the vicinity of airports. If you observe birds, deer, or other large animals in close proximity to movement areas, advise the FSS, tower, or airport management. Remote pilots should be aware of bird activity in proximity to their area of operation. It is well

Continued

documented that some types of birds are agitated by sUAS and may even attack such aircraft. Also, it has been shown that sUAS activity and noise may disturb certain types of wildlife; therefore remote pilots should be cognizant of the potential impact of their operations on the local environment. Many states are considering passing legislation to restrict sUAS operations that may disturb wildlife.

1130. Most midair collision accidents occur during

A— hazy days.
B— clear days.
C— cloudy nights.

The FAA Near Mid-Air Collision Report indicates that 81% of the incidents occurred in clear skies and unrestricted visibility conditions. (PLT526) — FAA-H-8083-25

1131. Which technique should a remote pilot use to scan for traffic?

A— Continuously scan the sky from right to left.
B— Concentrate on relative movement detected in the peripheral vision area.
C— Systematically focus on different segments of the sky for short intervals.

Effective scanning is accomplished with a series of short, regularly spaced eye movements that bring successive areas of the sky into the central visual field. Each movement should not exceed 10°, and each area should be observed for at least one second to enable detection. (PLT194) — AIM ¶8-1-6

1132. Guy wires, which support antenna towers, can extend horizontally; therefore, the towers should be avoided horizontally by at least

A— 2,000 feet horizontally.
B— 300 feet horizontally.
C— 1,000 feet horizontally.

Most skeletal structures are supported by guy wires which are very difficult to see in good weather and can be invisible at dusk or during periods of reduced visibility. These wires can extend about 1,500 feet horizontally from a structure; therefore, all skeletal structures should be avoided horizontally by at least 2,000 feet. (PLT194) — AIM ¶7-5-3

1133. What should remote pilots rely on for wire strike avoidance?

A— Sectional Chart markings.
B— *Chart Supplement U.S.* airport and airspace details.
C— Visual scanning.

The wire-rich environment is typically below 1,000 feet. Not all wires are marked and they can be nearly invisible when viewed from different angles. Remote pilots must exercise vigilance when operating near helicopters, moored balloons and other places where wires are frequently present. (PLT194) — SAFO 10015

1134. What should a remote pilot do if the sUAS they are operating collides with a bird or wildlife?

A— Report the collision to ATC.
B— File an accident report with the NTSB.
C— File a wildlife strike report with the FAA.

Remote pilots should report collisions between aircraft and wildlife to assist in the tracking of these incidents and to potentially mitigate future risks of these events. Reports may be sent to the FAA via their Wildlife Strike Report system (http://wildlife.faa.gov/strikenew.aspx). (PLT194) — AIM ¶7-4-5

1303. What is the most effective way for a UA pilot to scan for traffic?

A— Maintain your focus on the UA and use your peripheral vision to scan small segments of the sky.
B— A series of short regularly spaced eye movements scanning 10° segments of the sky.
C— Continuously scan the sky from right to left.

Effective scanning is accomplished with a series of short, regularly spaced eye movements that bring successive areas of the sky into the central visual field. Each movement should not exceed 10 degrees, and each area should be observed for at least one second to enable detection. (PLT194) — FAA-H-8083-25

Answers

| 1130 [B] | 1131 [C] | 1132 [A] | 1133 [C] | 1134 [C] | 1303 [B] |

1312. A larger UAS is converging head-on; what should you do?

A— The smaller aircraft should adjust course to the right.

B— The larger aircraft should adjust course to the right.

C— Both aircraft should adjust course to the right.

When aircraft are approaching each other head-on, or nearly so, each pilot of each aircraft (regardless of category or size) shall alter course to the right. (PLT414) — AC 107-2

Chapter 3
Weather

Introduction

As with any flight, the remote PIC should check and consider the weather conditions prior to and during every sUAS flight. Even though sUAS operations are often conducted at very low altitudes, weather factors can greatly influence performance and safety of flight. Specifically, factors that affect sUAS performance and risk management include:

- Atmospheric pressure and stability;

- Wind and currents;

- Uneven surface heating;

- Visibility and cloud clearance; and

- Precipitation.

The major source of all weather is the sun. Every physical process of weather, change or variation of weather patterns is accompanied by or is a result of unequal heating of the Earth's surface. The heating of the Earth (and therefore the heating of the air surrounding the Earth) is imbalanced around the entire planet. Both north and south of the equator, due to the different angle sunlight hits the Earth, one square foot of sunrays is not concentrated over one square foot of the surface, but over a larger area. This lower concentration of sunrays produces less radiation of heat over a given surface area; therefore, less atmospheric heating takes place in that area. The unequal heating of the Earth's atmosphere creates a large air-cell circulation pattern (wind) because the warmer air has a tendency to rise (associated with low pressure systems) and the colder air has a tendency to settle or descend (associated with high pressure systems) and replace the rising warmer air. This unequal heating, which causes pressure variations, will also cause variations in barometric altimeter settings between weather reporting points.

Different surfaces radiate heat in varying amounts. The resulting uneven heating of the air creates small areas of local circulation called convective currents. Convective currents can cause turbulent air that has the potential to dramatically affect the remote PIC's ability to control unmanned aircraft at lower altitudes. For example:

- Plowed ground, rocks, sand, barren land, pavement, and urban areas give off a large amount of heat and are likely to result in updrafts.

- Water, trees, and other areas of vegetation tend to absorb and retain heat and are likely to result in downdrafts.

1135. Which of the following considerations is most relevant to a remote PIC when evaluating unmanned aircraft performance?

A— Current weather conditions.
B— The number of available ground crew.
C— The type of sUAS operation.

Weather factors can greatly influence sUAS performance and safety of flight. (PLT510) — AC 107-2

1136. Every physical process of weather is accompanied by, or is the result of, a

A— movement of air.
B— pressure differential.
C— heat exchange.

Every physical process of weather is accompanied by, or is a result of, unequal heating of the Earth's surface. (PLT510) — AC 00-6

Answers
1135 [A]   1136 [C]

1137. What causes variations in altimeter settings between weather reporting points?

A— Unequal heating of the Earth's surface.
B— Variation of terrain elevation.
C— Coriolis force.

All altimeter settings are corrected to sea level. Unequal heating of the Earth's surface causes pressure differences. (PLT173) — AC 00-6

1138. The development of thermals depends upon

A— a counterclockwise circulation of air.
B— temperature inversions.
C— solar heating.

Thermals are updrafts in convective currents dependent on solar heating. A temperature inversion would result in stable air with very little, if any, convective activity. (PLT494) — AC 00-6

1139. (Refer to Figure 20.) Over which area should a Remote Pilot expect to find the highest amount of thermal currents under normal conditions?

A— 2.
B— 7.
C— 5.

Dry areas get hotter than moist areas. Dry fields or dry ground of any nature are better thermal sources than moist areas. This applies to woods or forests, which are poor sources of thermals because of the large amount of moisture given off by foliage. (PLT064) — AC 00-6

1272. Clouds, fog, or dew will always form when

A— water vapor condenses.
B— water vapor is present.
C— relative humidity reaches 100 percent.

As water vapor condenses or sublimates on condensation nuclei, liquid or ice particles begin to grow. Some condensation nuclei have an affinity for water and can induce condensation or sublimation even when air is almost, but not completely, saturated. (PLT345) — AC 00-6

Answer (B) is incorrect because the presence of water vapor does not result in clouds, fog, or dew unless condensation occurs. Answer (C) is incorrect because it is possible to have 100% humidity without the occurrence of condensation, which is necessary for clouds, fog, or dew to form.

Wind

Wind and currents can affect sUAS performance and maneuverability during all phases of flight. Be vigilant when operating sUAS at low altitudes, in confined areas, near buildings or other manmade structures, and near natural obstructions (such as mountains, bluffs, or canyons). Consider the following effects of wind on performance:

- Obstructions on the ground affect the flow of wind, may create rapidly changing wind speed and direction, and can be an unseen danger.

- High winds may make it difficult to maintain a geographical position in flight and may consume more battery power or preclude aircraft control and recovery.

Local conditions, geological features, and other anomalies can change the wind direction and speed close to the Earth's surface. For example, when operating close to a building, winds blowing against the building could cause strong updrafts that can result in ballooning or a loss of positive control. On the other hand, winds blowing over the building from the opposite side can cause significant downdrafts that can have a dramatic sinking effect on the unmanned aircraft that may exceed its climb performance.

The intensity of the turbulence associated with ground obstructions depends on the size of the obstacle and the primary velocity of the wind. This same condition is even more noticeable when flying in mountainous regions. While the wind flows smoothly up the windward side of the mountain and the upward currents help to carry an aircraft over the peak of the mountain, the wind on the leeward side

Answers

1137 [A]   1138 [C]   1139 [A]   1272 [A]

does not act in a similar manner. As the air flows down the leeward side of the mountain, the air follows the contour of the terrain and is increasingly turbulent. This tends to push an aircraft into the side of a mountain. The stronger the wind, the greater the downward pressure and turbulence become. Due to the effect terrain has on the wind in valleys or canyons, downdrafts can be severe. Even small hills or odd shaped terrain can have similar effects on local wind conditions. Remote pilots should be aware that terrain/object wind effects may exist for some distance downwind of the actual terrain or object.

1140. While operating around buildings, the remote PIC should be aware of the creation of wind gusts that

A— change rapidly in direction and speed causing turbulence.
B— enhance stability and imagery.
C— increase performance of the aircraft

Local conditions, geological features, and other anomalies can change the wind direction and speed close to the Earth's surface, making it difficult to control and maneuver the sUAS. (PLT198) — FAA-H-8083-25

1141. A strong steady wind exists out of the north. You need to photograph an area to the south of your location. You are located in an open field with no obstructions. Which of the following is not a concern during this operation?

A— Strong wind conditions may consume more battery power at a faster rate than in calm conditions.
B— Turbulent conditions will likely be a significant factor during the operation.
C— Strong wind may exceed the performance of the sUAS making it impossible to recover.

Unmanned aircraft often have limited performance and therefore in high wind conditions, it may consume more power to maintain position or other maneuvers than in calm air. If the wind is strong enough, the sUAS's performance might not be able to adequately counter the wind, making it difficult or impossible to fly back to you for recovery. (PLT198) — FAA-H-8083-25, 14 CFR §107.49

1278. Wind shear can exist

A— at all altitudes.
B— at low altitudes.
C— at high altitudes.

Wind shear is a sudden, drastic change in wind speed and/or direction over a very small area. Wind shear can subject an aircraft to violent updrafts and downdrafts, as well as abrupt changes to the horizontal movement of the aircraft. While wind shear can occur at any altitude, low-level wind shear is especially hazardous due to the proximity of an aircraft to the ground. (PLT192) — AC 00-6

Air Masses and Fronts

When a body of air comes to rest on, or moves slowly over, an extensive area having fairly uniform properties of temperature and moisture, the air takes on these properties. The area over which the air mass acquires its identifying distribution of temperature and moisture is its "source region." As this air mass moves from its source region, it tends to take on the properties of the new underlying surface. The trend toward change is called air mass modification. When an air mass that is different in such properties advances upon a dissimilar air mass, the division line is referred to as a front.

A ridge is an elongated area of high pressure. A trough is an elongated area of low pressure. All fronts lie in troughs. A cold front is the leading edge of an advancing cold air mass. Cold fronts are often accompanied by poor weather ahead of the front, which passes relatively quickly. Once the front has passed, there is a wind shift and, due to the increased wind speeds, turbulence is common for a period of time. More severe cold fronts can also produce thunderstorms, hail, and tornadoes.

A warm front is the leading edge of an advancing warm air mass. Warm fronts move about half as fast as cold fronts and have more widespread impact on weather. They are often preceded by lowered

Continued

Answers
1140 [A]   1141 [B]   1278 [A]

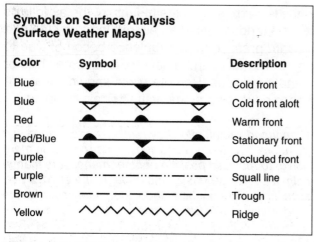

Figure 3-1. Weather map symbols

ceilings, increased precipitation, and reduced visibilities. Remote PICs should be aware of ambient and approaching weather systems as they can significantly impact their operations and safety of flight. Frontal waves and cyclones (areas of low pressure) usually form on slower-moving cold fronts or stationary fronts. These types of systems are often accompanied by conditions that may be unfavorable to sUAS operations. Figure 3-1 shows the symbols that would appear on a weather map.

The physical manifestations of a warm or cold front can be different with each front. They vary with the speed of the air mass on the move and the degree of stability of the air mass being overtaken. A stable air mass forced aloft will continue to exhibit stable characteristics, such as stratus clouds, calm air, steady precipitation, and poor visibility, while an unstable air mass forced to ascend will continue to be characterized by cumulus clouds, turbulence, showery precipitation, and good visibility.

Frontal passage will be indicated by the following discontinuities:

1. A temperature change (the most easily recognizable discontinuity);

2. A continuous decrease in pressure followed by an increase as the front passes; and

3. A shift in the wind direction, speed, or both.

1142. One of the most easily recognized discontinuities across a front is

A— a change in temperature.
B— an increase in cloud coverage.
C— an increase in relative humidity.

Temperature is one of the most easily recognized discontinuities across a front. (PLT511) — AC 00-6

Answer (B) is incorrect because cloud coverage is not always present across a front. Answer (C) is incorrect because relative humidity is not an easily recognized discontinuity across a front.

1143. One weather phenomenon which will always occur when flying across a front is a change in the

A— wind direction.
B— type of precipitation.
C— stability of the air mass.

Wind direction always changes across a front. (PLT511) — AC 00-6

Answer (B) is incorrect because precipitation does not always exist with a front. Answer (C) is incorrect because the stability on both sides of the front may be the same.

1144. Which type of weather phenomenon that may concern a remote pilot is common among cold fronts?

A— Long-term periods of reduced visibility.
B— Long periods of steady precipitation.
C— Thunderstorms and heavy rain.

Thunderstorms and heavy rain are common, although not always, associated with cold fronts. (PLT511) — AC 00-6

Answers (A) and (B) are incorrect because these characteristics would most typically be associated with warm fronts.

1286. What weather provides the best flying conditions?

A— Warm, moist air.
B— Cool, dry air.
C— Turbulence.

The combination of moisture and temperature determine the stability of the air and the resulting weather. Cool, dry air is very stable and resists vertical movement, which leads to good and generally clear weather. (PLT345) — AC 00-6

Answers

1142 [A]   1143 [A]   1144 [C]   1286 [B]

1277. The zone between different temperature, humidity, and wind is called

A— A front.
B— An air mass.
C— Wind shear.

The zone between two different air masses is a frontal zone or front. Across this zone, temperature, humidity and wind often change rapidly over short distances. (PLT345) — AC 00-6

Atmospheric Stability

Atmospheric stability is defined as the resistance of the atmosphere to vertical motion. A stable atmosphere resists any upward or downward movement. An unstable atmosphere allows an upward or downward disturbance to grow into a vertical (convective) current.

Determining the stability of the atmosphere requires measuring the difference between the actual existing (ambient) temperature lapse rate of a given parcel of air and the dry adiabatic (3°C per 1,000 feet) lapse rate. Because sUAS operate at low altitudes, it may seem as though lapse rate may not be a factor, but the stability of the local air mass can have significant impact on ambient conditions. Unstable air can often result in weather conditions unfavorable to sUAS operations.

A stable layer of air would be associated with a temperature inversion (a condition in which warm air is situated above cool or cold air). Warming from below, on the other hand, would decrease the stability of an air mass. The conditions shown in Figure 3-2 can be characteristic of stable or unstable air masses.

Unstable Air	Stable Air
Cumuliform clouds	Stratiform clouds and fog
Showery precipitation	Continuous precipitation
Rough air (turbulence)	Smooth air
Good visibility except in blowing obstructions	Fair to poor visibility in haze and smoke

Figure 3-2. Characteristics of stable and unstable air masses

1145. A stable air mass is most likely to have which characteristic?

A— Showery precipitation.
B— Turbulent air.
C— Poor surface visibility.

Characteristics of a stable air mass include stratiform clouds and fog, continuous precipitation, smooth air, and fair to poor visibility in haze and smoke. (PLT511) — FAA-H-8083-25

1146. What are characteristics of a moist, unstable air mass?

A— Turbulence and showery precipitation.
B— Poor visibility and smooth air.
C— Haze and smoke.

Characteristics of a moist, unstable air mass include cumuliform clouds, showery precipitation, rough air (turbulence), and good visibility (except in blowing obstructions). (PLT511) — AC 00-6

1147. What are characteristics of stable air?

A— Good visibility and steady precipitation.
B— Poor visibility and steady precipitation.
C— Poor visibility and intermittent precipitation.

Characteristics of a stable air mass include stratiform clouds and fog, continuous precipitation, smooth air, and fair to poor visibility in haze and smoke. (PLT511) — FAA-H-8083-25

Answers

1277 [A]	1145 [C]	1146 [A]	1147 [B]

1148. What measurement can be used to determine the stability of the atmosphere?

A— Atmospheric pressure.
B— Actual lapse rate.
C— Surface temperature.

The difference between the existing lapse rate of a given mass of air and the adiabatic rates of cooling in upward moving air determines if the air is stable or unstable. (PLT173) — AC 00-6

1149. What would decrease the stability of an air mass?

A— Warming from below.
B— Cooling from below.
C— Decrease in water vapor.

When air near the surface is warm and moist, suspect instability. Surface heating, cooling aloft, converging or upslope winds, or an invading mass of colder air may lead to instability and cumuliform clouds. (PLT173) — AC 00-6

Answer (B) is incorrect because cooling from the air below would increase the stability of the air. Answer (C) is incorrect because an increase in water vapor will result in a decrease in stability.

1150. Upon your preflight evaluation of weather, the forecasts you reference state there is an unstable air mass approaching your location. Which would not be a concern for your impending operation?

A— Thunderstorms.
B— Stratiform clouds.
C— Turbulent conditions.

Unstable conditions are characterized by cumulus clouds, turbulence, showery precipitation, and good visibility. (PLT511) — AC 00-6

1285. You have received an outlook briefing from flight service through 1800wxbrief.com. The briefing indicates you can expect a low-level temperature inversion with high relative humidity. What weather conditions would you expect?

A— Smooth air, poor visibility, fog, haze, or low clouds.
B— Light wind shear, poor visibility, haze, and light rain.
C— Turbulent air, poor visibility, fog, low stratus type clouds, and showery precipitation.

When the temperature of the air rises with altitude, a temperature inversion exists. Inversion layers are commonly shallow layers of smooth, stable air close to the ground. The temperature of the air increases with altitude to a certain point, which is the top of the inversion. The air at the top of the layer acts as a lid, keeping weather and pollutants trapped below. If the relative humidity of the air is high, it can contribute to the formation of clouds, fog, haze, or smoke resulting in diminished visibility in the inversion layer. (PLT301) — AC 00-6

Visibility and Clouds

As in manned aircraft operations, good visibility and safe distance from clouds enhances the remote PIC's ability to see and avoid other aircraft. Similarly, good visibility and cloud clearance may be the only means for other aircraft to see and avoid the unmanned aircraft. Prior to flight, the remote PIC must determine that visibility from the control station (CS) is at least 3 SM and that the sUAS is kept at least 500 feet below a cloud and at least 2,000 feet horizontally from a cloud. These standards must be maintained throughout flight operations.

One of the ways to ensure adherence to the minimum visibility and cloud clearance requirements is to obtain local aviation weather reports that include current and forecast weather conditions. If there is more than one local aviation reporting station near the operating area, the remote PIC should choose the closest one that is also the most representative of the terrain surrounding the operating area. If local aviation weather reports are not available, then the remote PIC may not operate the small UA if he or she is unable to determine the required visibility and cloud clearances by other reliable means.

Answers

1148 [B]   1149 [A]   1150 [B]   1285 [A]

The remote pilot can determine local visibility by verifying that a known point at least 3 SM away is visible. Similarly, an object with a known height can be observed to have clouds above that object, providing information about how much operational altitude is available for use. For example, you know a nearby tower extends to 1,000 AGL (referencing a Sectional Chart). The clouds are above the top. Thus you know that even if you climb to the maximum altitude of 400 AGL, you have more than the required 500 feet of separation from the clouds. When in doubt always choose the most conservative and safest option, which sometimes may be to delay the operation. It is imperative that the UA not be operated above any cloud, and that there are no obstructions to visibility, such as smoke or a cloud, between the UA and the remote PIC.

1151. What minimum visibility is required for sUAS operations?

A— 1 miles.
B— 3 miles.
C— 4 miles.

Crewmembers must operate sUAS Part 107 operations with a minimum visibility, as observed from the location of the control station, no less than 3 statute miles. (PLT163) — 14 CFR §107.51

1152. The minimum distance from clouds required for sUAS Part 107 operations is

A— clear of clouds.
B— 500 feet below, 2,000 feet horizontally.
C— 500 feet above, 1,000 feet horizontally.

Part 107 sUAS operations require the minimum distance of the small unmanned aircraft from clouds must be no less than 500 feet below the cloud and 2,000 feet horizontally from the cloud. (PLT163) — 14 CFR §107.51

1288. (Refer to Figure 69.) You are inspecting the lighted towers approximately 8 NM SW of the Corpus Christi Intl airport (CRP). What is the lowest cloud cover that will enable you to inspect the top of the tower?

A— 1,104 feet MSL.
B— 1,604 feet MSL.
C— 1,054 feet MSL.

Part 107 requires that the minimum distance of the sUAS from clouds must be no less than 500 feet below the cloud. The towers depicted 8 NM SW of CRP are 1,104 feet MSL. 1,104 + 500 = 1,604 feet MSL. (PLT163) — 14 CFR §107.51

1271. The weather report lists the ceiling at 800 feet. What is the highest you can operate your sUAS?

A— 200 feet AGL.
B— 800 feet AGL.
C— 300 feet AGL.

Part 107 requires that the minimum distance of the sUAS from clouds must be no less than 500 feet below the cloud. 800 cloud – 500 = 300 feet AGL. (PLT163) — 14 CFR §107.51

1289. (Refer to Figure 23.) What are the VFR minimum visibility requirements over Plantation Airport?

A— 1 SM.
B— 5 SM.
C— 3 SM.

Regardless of the location, crewmembers must conduct sUAS Part 107 operations with a minimum visibility, as observed from the location of the control station, no less than 3 statute miles. (PLT163) — 14 CFR §107.51

1310. (Refer to Figure 78.) What is the minimum base of the cloud layer to fly to the top of the towers 4 NM east of Onawa (K36)?

A— 792 feet AGL.
B— 292 feet AGL.
C— 1,335 feet MSL.

Part 107 requires that the minimum distance of the sUAS from clouds must be no less than 500 feet below the cloud. The towers depicted 4 NM east of K36 are 292 feet AGL. 292 + 500 = 792 feet AGL. (PLT163) — 14 CFR §107.51

Answers

1151 [B]	1152 [B]	1288 [B]	1271 [C]	1289 [C]	1310 [A]

Thunderstorms

Thunderstorms present many hazards to flying. Three conditions necessary for the formation of a thunderstorm are:

1. Sufficient water vapor;
2. An unstable lapse rate; and
3. An initial lifting force (upward boost).

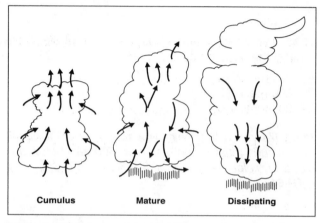

Figure 3-3. Stages of thunderstorms

The lifting action can be caused by heating from below, frontal lifting, or by mechanical lifting (wind blowing air upslope on a mountain). There are three stages of a thunderstorm: the cumulus, mature, and dissipating stages. *See* Figure 3-3.

The cumulus stage is characterized by continuous updrafts, and these updrafts create low-pressure areas. Thunderstorms reach their greatest intensity during the mature stage, which is characterized by updrafts and downdrafts inside the cloud. Precipitation inside the cloud aids in the development of these downdrafts, and the start of rain from the base of the cloud signals the beginning of the mature stage. The precipitation that evaporates before it reaches the ground is called virga. Virga is typically associated with very turbulent conditions and should be avoided. The dissipating stage of a thunderstorm is characterized predominantly by downdrafts.

Lightning is always associated with a thunderstorm. The frequency of lightning is a good indicator of the severity of the storm. Upon observing frequent nearby lightning, remote PICs should recover their crew and sUAS in order to seek cover. One way to determine the distance a storm is from your location is to count the number of seconds it takes between when you see lightning and then hear thunder. Take the result and divide by 5 to give you the distance in statute miles (SM). If there is frequent lightning or multiple storms, this method may not be feasible. Ideally, remote pilots can monitor the weather by electronic means and observe incoming systems with precise detail.

Hail is formed inside thunderstorms by the constant freezing, melting, and refreezing of water as it is carried about by the up- and downdrafts.

Thunderstorms that generally produce the most intense hazard to aircraft are called squall-line thunderstorms. These non-frontal, narrow bands of thunderstorms often develop ahead of a cold front. Embedded thunderstorms are those that are obscured by massive cloud layers and cannot be seen. A pilot should always expect the hazardous and invisible atmospheric phenomena called wind shear turbulence when operating anywhere near a thunderstorm (within 20 NM).

Microbursts are small-scale intense downdrafts which, as they get near the ground, spread outward from the center in all directions. Maximum downdrafts at the center of a microburst may be as strong as 6,000 feet per minute far exceeding the capabilities of sUAS. Also, wind speeds in excess of 45 knots and shears of 90 knots or more may exist which may cause an upset or loss of control of an sUAS. An individual microburst will seldom last longer than 15 minutes from the time it strikes the ground until dissipation. The horizontal winds continue to increase during the first 5 minutes with the maximum intensity winds and last approximately 2 – 4 minutes.

The most violent thunderstorms draw air into their cloud bases with great vigor. If the incoming air has any initial rotating motion, it often forms an extremely concentrated vortex from the surface well into the cloud. Meteorologists have estimated that wind in such a vortex can exceed 200 knots with pressure inside the vortex quite low. The strong winds gather dust and debris and the low pressure generates a funnel-shaped cloud extending downward from the cumulonimbus base. If the cloud does not reach the surface, it is a funnel cloud; if it touches a land surface, it is a tornado. Tornadoes occur with both isolated and squall line thunderstorms. Remote pilots should avoid operations during or in close proximity to thunderstorm activity, especially those that appear to be severe.

Remote pilots should be aware that some phenomenon (e.g. hail, lightning, windshear, and microbursts) can occur well away from the center of the storm. Extreme caution is advised when operating in conditions that may generate thunderstorms.

1153. What feature is normally associated with the cumulus stage of a thunderstorm?

A— Roll cloud.
B— Continuous updraft.
C— Frequent lightning.

The key feature of the cumulus stage is an updraft. Precipitation beginning to fall from the cloudbase is the signal that a downdraft has developed also and a cell has entered the mature stage. (PLT495) — AC 00-6

Answer (A) is incorrect because a roll cloud is associated with a mountain wave. Answer (C) is incorrect because frequent lightning may be present in any stage.

1154. Which weather phenomenon signals the beginning of the mature stage of a thunderstorm?

A— The appearance of an anvil top.
B— Precipitation beginning to fall.
C— Maximum growth rate of the clouds.

The key feature of the cumulus stage is an updraft. Precipitation beginning to fall from the cloudbase is the signal that a downdraft has developed also and the cell has entered the mature stage. (PLT495) — AC 00-6

Answer (A) is incorrect because the appearance of an anvil top is characteristic of the dissipating stage. Answer (C) is incorrect because the maximum growth rate of the clouds is during the mature stage of a thunderstorm, but it does not signal the beginning of that stage.

1155. What conditions are necessary for the formation of thunderstorms?

A— High humidity, lifting force, and unstable conditions.
B— High humidity, high temperature, and cumulus clouds.
C— Lifting force, moist air, and extensive cloud cover.

For a cumulonimbus cloud or thunderstorm to form, the air must have:

1. *Sufficient water vapor,*

2. *An unstable lapse rate, and*

3. *An initial upward boost (lifting) to start the storm process in motion.*

(PLT495) — AC 00-6

1156. During the life cycle of a thunderstorm, which stage is characterized predominately by downdrafts?

A— Cumulus.
B— Dissipating.
C— Mature.

Downdrafts characterize the dissipating stage of the thunderstorm cell and the storm dies rapidly. (PLT495) — AC 00-6

Answer (A) is incorrect because updrafts occur during the cumulus stage. Answer (C) is incorrect because both updrafts and downdrafts occur during the mature stage.

1157. Thunderstorms reach their greatest intensity during the

A— mature stage.
B— downdraft stage.
C— cumulus stage.

All thunderstorm hazards reach their greatest intensity during the mature stage. (PLT495) — AC 00-6

Answers

| 1153 [B] | 1154 [B] | 1155 [A] | 1156 [B] | 1157 [A] |

1158. Thunderstorms which generally produce the most intense hazard to aircraft are

A— squall line thunderstorms.
B— steady-state thunderstorms.
C— warm front thunderstorms.

A squall line is a non-frontal, narrow band of active thunderstorms. The line may be too long to easily detour and too wide and severe to penetrate. It often contains severe steady-state thunderstorms and presents the single, most intense weather hazard to aircraft. (PLT495) — AC 00-6

1159. A nonfrontal, narrow band of active thunderstorms that often develop ahead of a cold front is known as a

A— prefrontal system.
B— squall line.
C— dry line.

A squall line is a nonfrontal, narrow band of active thunderstorms. The line may be too long to easily detour and too wide and severe to penetrate. It often contains severe steady-state thunderstorms and presents the single, most intense weather hazard to aircraft. (PLT495) — AC 00-6

1160. If there is thunderstorm activity in the vicinity of an airport at which you plan to land, which hazardous atmospheric phenomenon might be expected during recovery/landing of the sUAS?

A— Precipitation static.
B— Wind-shear turbulence.
C— Steady rain.

Wind shear is an invisible hazard associated with all thunderstorms. Shear turbulence has been encountered 20 miles laterally from a severe storm. (PLT495) — AC 00-6

Answer (A) is incorrect because precipitation static is not considered a hazardous atmospheric phenomenon. Answer (C) is incorrect because showery precipitation is a characteristic of thunderstorm activity.

1161. Which weather phenomenon is always associated with a thunderstorm?

A— Lightning.
B— Heavy rain.
C— Hail.

A thunderstorm is, in general, a local storm invariably produced by a cumulonimbus cloud, and is always accompanied by lightning and thunder. (PLT495) — AC 00-6

1162. Which is considered to be the most hazardous condition when flying an sUAS in the vicinity of thunderstorms?

A— Static electricity.
B— Lightning.
C— Wind shear and turbulence.

During the mature stage of a thunderstorm, updrafts and downdrafts in close proximity create strong vertical shears and a very turbulent environment. A lightning strike can puncture the skin of an aircraft, damage communication and navigation equipment, or hit the remote pilot or crew on the ground. (PLT495) — AC 00-6

1163. What is the expected duration of an individual microburst?

A— Two minutes with maximum winds lasting approximately 1 minute.
B— One microburst may continue for as long as 2 to 4 hours.
C— Seldom longer than 15 minutes from the time the burst strikes the ground until dissipation.

An individual microburst will seldom last longer than 15 minutes from the time it strikes the ground until dissipation. However, there may be multiple microbursts in the area. (PLT495) — AIM ¶7-1-25

1283. In what stage are thunderstorms the strongest?

A— Mature.
B— Dissipating.
C— Cumulus.

Thunderstorm hazards reach their greatest intensity during the mature stage, which is when precipitation begins. (PLT192) — AC 00-6

1287. Where are squalls most likely to form?

A— High altitude.
B— Low altitude.
C— At any altitude.

A continuous line of thunderstorms, or squall line, may form along or ahead of the front. Squall lines present a serious hazard to pilots as squall type thunderstorms are intense and move quickly. Squalls can occur at any altitude—they are not unique to high- or low-altitude operations. (PLT192) — AC 00-6

Answers

1158 [A]	1159 [B]	1160 [B]	1161 [A]	1162 [B]	1163 [C]
1283 [A]	1287 [C]				

Icing

Structural icing occurs on an aircraft whenever supercooled condensed droplets of water make contact with any part of the aircraft that is also at a temperature below freezing. An inflight condition necessary for structural icing to form is visible moisture (clouds or raindrops). Icing in precipitation (rain) is of concern to the remote pilot because it can occur outside of clouds. Aircraft structural ice will most likely have the highest accumulation in freezing rain which indicates warmer temperature at a higher altitude. The effects of structural icing on an sUAS are as follows:

- Lift decreases;
- Weight and stalling speed increase for fixed wing, and propellers may stall on rotary wing;
- Thrust decreases; and
- Drag increases.

The presence of ice pellets at the surface is evidence that there is freezing rain at a higher altitude, while wet snow indicates that the temperature at your altitude is above freezing. A situation conducive to any icing would be flying in the vicinity of a front.

Remote pilots should avoid flight in conditions that may produce icing. If it appears that ice is accumulating on the sUAS, it should be recovered immediately to avoid loss of control.

1164. The presence of ice pellets at the surface is evidence that there

A— are thunderstorms in the area.
B— has been cold frontal passage.
C— is a temperature inversion with freezing rain at a higher altitude.

Ice pellets always indicate freezing rain at higher altitude. (PLT263) — AC 00-6

1165. One in-flight condition necessary for structural icing to form is

A— small temperature/dewpoint spread.
B— stratiform clouds.
C— visible moisture.

Two conditions are necessary for structural icing in flight:

1. *The aircraft must be flying through visible water such as rain or cloud droplets, and*

2. *The temperature at the point where the moisture strikes the aircraft must be 0°C (32°F) or colder.*

(PLT263) — AC 00-6

1166. In which environment is aircraft structural ice most likely to have the highest accumulation rate?

A— Cumulus clouds with below freezing temperatures.
B— Freezing drizzle.
C— Freezing rain.

A condition favorable for rapid accumulation of clear icing is freezing rain below a frontal surface. (PLT263) — AC 00-6

Answers (A) and (B) are incorrect because although cumulus clouds with below-freezing temperatures and freezing drizzle are conducive to structural icing, they will not have as high an accumulation rate as freezing rain.

1298. What environment is most conducive to frost formation?

A— Dewpoint of surface is below freezing, dewpoint is above freezing.

B— Surface temperature is below freezing, air temperature is below freezing.

C— Surface temperature is above freezing, air temperature is below freezing.

On cool, clear, calm nights, the temperature of the ground and objects on the surface can cause temperatures of the surrounding air to drop below the dew point. When this occurs, the moisture in the air condenses and deposits itself on the ground, buildings, and other objects like cars and aircraft. This moisture is known as dew and sometimes can be seen on grass and other objects in the morning. If the temperature is below freezing, the moisture is deposited in the form of frost. (PLT345) — AC 00-6

Fog

Fog is a surface-based cloud (restricting visibility) composed of either water droplets or ice crystals. Fog may form by cooling the air to its dew point or by adding moisture to the air near the ground. A small temperature/dew point spread is essential to the formation of fog. An abundance of condensation nuclei from combustion products makes fog prevalent in industrial areas.

Fog is classified by the way it is formed:

• **Radiation fog** (ground fog) is formed when terrestrial radiation cools the ground, which in turn cools the air in contact with it. When the air is cooled to its dew point (or within a few degrees), fog will form. This fog will form most readily in warm, moist air over low, flatland areas on clear, calm (no wind) nights.

• **Advection fog** (sea fog) is formed when warm, moist air moves (wind is required) over colder ground or water (e.g., an air mass moving inland from the coast in winter).

• **Upslope fog** is formed when moist, stable air is cooled to its dew point as it moves up along sloping terrain (wind is required). Cooling will be at the dry adiabatic lapse rate of approximately 3°C per 1,000 feet.

Precipitation (rain or drizzle)-induced fog is most commonly associated with frontal activity and is formed by relatively warm drizzle or rain falling through cooler air. Evaporation from the precipitation saturates the cool air and fog forms. This fog is especially critical because it occurs in the proximity of precipitation and other possible hazards such as icing, turbulence, and thunderstorms.

Steam fog forms in the winter when cold, dry air passes from land areas over comparatively warm ocean waters. Low-level turbulence can occur and icing can become hazardous in a steam fog.

Remote pilots should be cautious when conditions are conducive to the formation of fog (e.g., when temperature and dew points are converging), especially at dusk or before dawn. Visibility can rapidly change once fog begins to form. The sUAS should be recovered if visibility approaches the 3 SM minimum.

1167. What situation is most conducive to the formation of radiation fog?

A— Warm, moist air over low, flatland areas on clear, calm nights.

B— Moist, tropical air moving over cold, offshore water.

C— The movement of cold air over much warmer water.

Conditions favorable for radiation fog are clear sky, little or no wind, and small temperature/dew point spread (high relative humidity). Radiation fog is restricted to land because water surfaces cool little from nighttime radiation. (PLT226) — AC 00-6

Answers (B) and (C) are incorrect because radiation fog will not form over water since water surfaces cool little from nighttime radiation.

Answers

1298 [A]   1167 [A]

1168. In which situation is advection fog most likely to form?

A— A warm, moist air mass on the windward side of mountains.

B— An air mass moving inland from the coast in winter.

C— A light breeze blowing colder air out to sea.

Advection fog forms when moist air moves over colder ground or water. It is most common along coastal areas. This fog frequently forms offshore as a result of cold water, then is carried inland by the wind. (PLT226) — AC 00-6

Answer (A) is incorrect because a warm, moist air mass on the windward side of mountains will form upslope fog and/or rain. Answer (C) is incorrect because a light breeze blowing colder air out to sea will form steam fog.

1169. An air mass moving inland from the coast in winter is likely to result in

A— rain.

B— fog.

C— frost.

Advection fog forms when moist air moves over colder ground or water. It is most common along coastal areas. This fog frequently forms offshore as a result of cold water, then is carried inland by the wind. (PLT226) — AC 00-6

1170. What types of fog depend upon wind in order to exist?

A— Radiation fog and ice fog.

B— Steam fog and ground fog.

C— Advection fog and upslope fog.

Advection fog forms when moist air moves over colder ground or water. It is most common along coastal areas, but often develops deep in continental areas. Advection fog deepens as wind speed increases up to about 15 knots. Wind much stronger than 15 knots lifts the fog into a layer of low stratus or stratocumulus. Upslope fog forms as a result of moist, stable air being cooled adiabatically as it moves up sloping terrain. Once upslope wind ceases, the fog dissipates. (PLT226) — AC 00-6

Answer (A) is incorrect because radiation fog and ice fog do not depend upon wind in order to exist. Answer (B) is incorrect because ground fog does not depend on wind in order to exist.

1171. Low-level turbulence can occur and icing can become hazardous in which type of fog?

A— Rain-induced fog.

B— Upslope fog.

C— Steam fog.

Steam fog forms in the winter when cold, dry air passes from land areas over comparatively warm ocean waters. Low-level turbulence can occur and icing can become hazardous in a steam fog. (PLT226) — AC 00-6

1172. What is the best way for a remote pilot to determine the likelihood of local fog formation?

A— Monitor the temperature/dew point spread.

B— Monitor the wind conditions to insure the wind speed is not increasing.

C— Monitor the barometric pressure to insure that it is not decreasing.

Fog is more likely to form when the temperature and dew point converge. A difference between these two temperatures of 3°C (or 5°F) is indicative of possible fog formation. (PLT226) — AC 00-6

Density Altitude

Manufacturer performance information conveys to the remote pilot what can be expected of an sUAS (rate of climb, takeoff roll, etc.) under ideal conditions. Prediction of performance is based upon the conditions a manufacturer chooses, but is often similar to manned aircraft calculations which use a sea level temperature of +15°C (+59°F) and atmospheric pressure of 29.92" Hg (1013.2 mb). This combination of temperature and pressure is called a "standard day." When the air is at a "standard density," temperature and/or pressure deviations from standard will change the air density, or the density altitude, and that change affects sUAS performance. Remote pilots should be aware that conditions which deviate away from the manufacturer-calculated or standard conditions will impact performance.

Continued

Answers

1168 [B]   1169 [B]   1170 [C]   1171 [C]   1172 [A]

Relative humidity also affects density altitude, but should have minimal impact on sUAS performance. Overall, sUAS flight performance will decrease as atmospheric pressure decreases, altitude increases (in flight or at higher launch sites), temperature increases, and marginally with increased humidity. A combination of high temperature, high humidity, and high altitude result in a density altitude higher than the pressure altitude which, in turn, results in reduced aircraft performance.

1173. How would high density altitude affect the performance of a small unmanned aircraft?

A— No change in performance.
B— Increased performance.
C— Decreased performance.

A combination of high temperature, high humidity, and high altitude result in a density altitude higher than the pressure altitude which, in turn, results in reduced aircraft performance. (PLT127) — FAA-H-8083-25

1174. If the outside air temperature (OAT) at a given altitude is warmer than standard, the density altitude is

A— equal to pressure altitude.
B— lower than pressure altitude.
C— higher than pressure altitude.

If the temperature is above standard, the density altitude will be higher than pressure altitude. (PLT127) — FAA-H-8083-25

1175. What are the standard temperature and pressure values for sea level?

A— 15°C and 29.92" Hg.
B— 59°C and 1013.2 millibars.
C— 59°F and 29.92 millibars.

Standard sea level pressure is 29.92 inches of mercury. Standard sea level temperature is 15°C. (PLT345) — FAA-H-8083-25

1176. Which factor would tend to increase the density altitude at a given airport referenced in the weather briefing?

A— An increase in barometric pressure.
B— An increase in ambient temperature.
C— A decrease in relative humidity.

On a hot day, the air becomes "thinner" or lighter, and its density is equivalent to a higher altitude in the standard atmosphere, thus the term "high density altitude." (PLT206) — AC 00-6

Answer (A) is incorrect because an increase in barometric pressure would decrease density altitude. Answer (C) is incorrect because a decrease in relative humidity would decrease density altitude.

1177. What effect does high density altitude have on the efficiency of a UA propeller?

A— Propeller efficiency is increased.
B— Propeller efficiency is decreased.
C— Density altitude does not affect propeller efficiency.

The propeller produces thrust in proportion to the mass of air being accelerated through the rotating blades. If the air is less dense, propeller efficiency is decreased. (PLT351) — FAA-H-8083-25

1290. What effect does humidity have on performance?

A— It has no effect on performance.
B— It increases performance.
C— It decreases performance.

An increase in air temperature or humidity, or a decrease in air pressure (which results in a higher density altitude) will significantly decrease both power output and propeller efficiency. If an air mass is humid, there is more water in it, therefore, less oxygen. (PLT124) — AC 00-6

Weather Briefing

Remote PICs are encouraged to obtain weather information from Flight Service prior to flight by visiting **www.1800wxbrief.com**. Remote PICs can create a free account in order to use the briefing service. While Flight Service does offer a telephone-based service, it is intended for manned aircraft pilots only.

Remote PICs are also encouraged to visit the **NWS Aviation Weather Center (AWC)** at **www.aviationweather.gov**. This free, web-based service does not require registration and offers all of the weather products important to a remote PIC, such as **Aviation Routine Weather Reports (METAR)** and **Terminal Aerodrome Forecast (TAF)**. While reviewing the weather for your intended operation, it is also critical that the remote PIC review any temporary flight restrictions (TFR) at the FAA's TFR website at **http://tfr.faa.gov**.

Request a standard briefing to get a "complete" weather briefing. Request an abbreviated briefing to supplement mass disseminated data or when only one or two items are needed. Request an outlook briefing whenever the proposed departure time is 6 or more hours from the time of briefing.

Remote pilots need to learn the various abbreviations and symbols of textual weather reports in order to interpret them properly, and should familiarize themselves with available graphical products to be able to understand available weather maps and images.

1178. To get a complete weather overview for the planned flight, the remote pilot in command should obtain

A— An outlook briefing.
B— An abbreviated briefing.
C— A standard briefing.

You should request a standard briefing any time you are planning a flight and you have not received a previous briefing. (PLT514) — FAA-H-8083-25

Weather Reports, Forecasts and Charts

Remote pilots can access weather reports, forecasts and charts by visiting **www.aviationweather.gov** or **www.1800wxbrief.com**.

The **Automated Surface Observing System (ASOS)** is the primary surface weather observing system of the U.S. Automated weather reporting systems are increasingly being installed at airports. These systems consist of various sensors, a processor, a computer-generated voice subsystem, and a transmitter to broadcast local, minute-by-minute weather data directly to the pilot. The **Automated Weather Observing System (AWOS)** observations will include the prefix "AUTO" to indicate that the data is derived from an automated system.

An international weather reporting code is used for weather reports (METAR) and forecasts (TAFs) worldwide. The reports follow the format shown in Figure 3-4. For aviation purposes, the ceiling is the lowest broken or overcast layer, or vertical visibility into an obscuration.

Surface Aviation Weather Observations

Surface aviation weather observations are a compilation of elements of the current weather at individual ground stations across the United States. The network is made up of government and privately contracted facilities that provide continuous up-to-date weather information. Automated weather sources, such as the Automated Weather Observing Systems (AWOS), Automated Surface Observing Systems (ASOS), as well as other automated facilities, also play a major role in the gathering of surface observations.

Answers
1178 [C]

Surface observations provide local weather conditions and other relevant information for a specific airport. This information includes the type of report, station identifier, date and time, modifier (as required), wind, visibility, runway visual range (RVR), weather phenomena, sky condition, temperature/dew point, altimeter reading, and applicable remarks. The information gathered for the surface observation may be from a person, an automated station, or an automated station that is updated or enhanced by a weather observer. In any form, the surface observation provides valuable information about individual airports around the country. These reports cover a small area and will be beneficial to the remote pilot.

Aviation Weather Reports

Aviation weather reports are designed to give accurate depictions of current weather conditions. Each report provides current information that is updated at different times. Some typical reports are METARs and PIREPs. To view a weather report, go to **http://www.aviationweather.gov/**.

Key to Aerodrome Forecast (TAF) and Aviation Routine Weather Report (METAR)

```
TAF    KPIT 091730Z 0918/1024 15005KT 5SM HZ FEW020 WS010/31022KT
       FM091930 30015G25KT 3SM SHRA OVC015
       TEMPO 0920/0922 1/2SM +TSRA OVC008CB
       FM100100 27008KT 5SM SHRA BKN020 OVC040
       PROB30 1004/1007 1SM -RA BR
       FM101015 18005KT 6SM -SHRA OVC020
       BECMG 1013/1015 P6SM NSW SKC
```

Note: Users are cautioned to confirm *DATE* and *TIME* of the TAF.
For example FM**100000** is 0000Z on the **10th**. Do not confuse with *1000Z*!

METAR KPIT 091955Z COR 22015G25KT 3/4SM R28L/2600FT TSRA OVC010CB
18/16 A2992 RMK SLP045 T01820159

Forecast	Explanation	Report
TAF	Message type: <u>TAF</u>: routine or TAF <u>AMD</u>: amended forecast; <u>METAR</u>: hourly; <u>SPECI</u>: special or <u>TESTM</u>: noncommissioned ASOS report	METAR
KPIT	ICAO location indicator	KPIT
091730Z	Issuance time: ALL times in UTC "<u>Z</u>", 2-digit date, 4-digit time	091955Z
0918/1024	Valid period: Either 24 hours or 30 hours. The first two digits of EACH four-digit number indicate the date of the valid period, the final two digits indicate the time (valid from 18Z on the 9th to 24Z on the 10th).	
	In U.S. **METAR**: <u>COR</u>rected ob; or <u>AUTO</u>mated ob for automated report with no human intervention; omitted when observer logs on.	COR
15005KT	Wind: 3-digit true-north direction, nearest 10 degrees (or <u>VaRiaBle</u>); next 2–3 digits for speed and unit, <u>KT</u> (KMH or MPS); as needed, <u>G</u>ust and maximum speed; 00000KT for calm; for **METAR**, if direction varies 60 degrees or more, <u>V</u>ariability appended, e.g., 180<u>V</u>260	22015G25KT
5SM	Prevailing visibility: In U.S., <u>S</u>tatute Miles and fractions; above 6 miles in **TAF** <u>Plus6SM</u>. (Or, 4-digit minimum visibility in meters and as required, lowest value with direction).	3/4SM
	Runway Visual Range: <u>R</u>; 2-digit runway designator <u>L</u>eft, <u>C</u>enter, or <u>R</u>ight as needed; "<u>/</u>"; <u>M</u>inus or <u>P</u>lus in U.S., 4-digit value, <u>Fee</u>T in U.S. (usually meters elsewhere); 4-digit value <u>V</u>ariability, 4-digit value (and tendency <u>D</u>own, <u>U</u>p or <u>N</u>o change)	R28L/2600FT
HZ	Significant present, forecast and recent weather: See table (to the right)	TSRA
FEW020	Cloud amount, height and type: <u>SK</u>y <u>C</u>lear 0/8, <u>FEW</u> >0/8-2/8, <u>SCa</u>ttered 3/8-4/8, <u>Bro</u>Ke<u>N</u> 5/8-7/8, <u>O</u>Ver<u>C</u>ast 8/8; 3-digit height in hundreds of feet; <u>T</u>owering <u>CU</u>mulus or <u>Cumulonim</u>Bus in **METAR**; in **TAF**, only <u>CB</u>. <u>V</u>ertical <u>V</u>isibility for obscured sky and height "VV004". More than 1 layer may be reported or forecast. In automated **METAR** reports only, <u>CL</u>ea<u>R</u> for "clear below 12,000 feet."	OVC010CB
	Temperature: Degrees Celsius; first 2 digits, temperature "<u>/</u>" last 2 digits, dewpoint temperature; <u>M</u>inus for below zero, e.g., M06	18/16
	Altimeter setting: Indicator and 4 digits; in U.S., <u>A</u>: inches and hundredths; (<u>Q</u>: hectoPascals, e.g., Q1013)	A2992
	Continued	

Figure 3-4. TAF/METAR weather card

Key to Aerodrome Forecast (TAF) and Aviation Routine Weather Report (METAR)

Forecast	Explanation	Report
WS010/ 31022KT	In U.S. **TAF**, nonconvective low-level (≤2,000 feet) <u>W</u>ind <u>S</u>hear; 3-digit height (hundreds of feet); "<u>/</u>"; 3-digit wind direction and 2–3 digit wind speed above the indicated height, and unit, <u>KT</u>	
	In **METAR**, <u>ReMarK</u> indicator and remarks. For example: <u>S</u>ea-<u>L</u>evel <u>P</u>ressure in hectoPascals and tenths, as shown: 1004.5 hPa; <u>Temp</u>/ dewpoint in tenths °C, as shown: temp. 18.2°C, dewpoint 15.9°C	RMK SLP045 T01820159
FM091930	<u>FroM</u>: Changes are expected at: 2-digit date, 2-digit hour, and 2-digit minute **beginning** time: indicates significant change. Each FM starts on a new line, indented 5 spaces	
TEMPO 0920/0922	<u>TEMPO</u>rary: Changes expected for <1 hour and in total, < half of the period between the 2-digit date and 2-digit hour **beginning**, and 2-digit date and 2-digit hour **ending** time	
PROB30 1004/1007	<u>PROB</u>ability and 2-digit percent (30 or 40): Probable condition in the period between the 2-digit date and 2-digit hour **beginning** time, and the 2-digit date and 2-digit hour **ending** time	
BECMG 1013/1015	<u>BECoMinG</u>: Change expected in the period between the 2-digit date and 2-digit hour **beginning** time, and the 2-digit date and 2-digit hour **ending** time	

Table of Significant Present, Forecast and Recent Weather – Grouped in categories and used in the order listed below; or as needed in TAF, <u>No Significant Weather</u>

QUALIFIERS
Intensity or Proximity
"–" = Light   **No sign** = Moderate   "+" = Heavy

"**VC**" = Vicinity, but not at aerodrome. In the U.S. **METAR**, 5 to 10 SM from the point of observation. In the U.S. **TAF**, 5 to 10 SM from the center of the runway complex. Elsewhere, within 8000m.

Descriptor

BC	Patches	**BL**	Blowing	**DR**	Drifting	**FZ**	Freezing
MI	Shallow	**PR**	Partial	**SH**	Showers	**TS**	Thunderstorm

WEATHER PHENOMENA
Precipitation

DZ	Drizzle	**GR**	Hail			**GS**	Small hail or snow pellets
IC	Ice crystals	**PL**	Ice pellets			**RA**	Rain	**SG**	Snow grains
SN	Snow	**UP**	Unknown precipitation in automated observations				

Obscuration

BR	Mist (≥5/8SM)	**DU**	Widespread dust	**FG**	Fog (<5/8SM)	**FU**	Smoke
HZ	Haze	**PY**	Spray	**SA**	Sand	**VA**	Volcanic ash

Other

DS	Dust storm	**FC**	Funnel cloud	**+FC**	Tornado or waterspout		
PO	Well-developed dust or sand whirls	**SQ**	Squall	**SS**	Sandstorm		

• Explanations in parentheses "( )" indicate different worldwide practices.
• Ceiling is not specified; defined as the lowest broken or overcast layer, or the vertical visibility.
• NWS **TAFs** exclude BECMG groups and temperature forecasts, NWS TAFs do not use PROB in the first 9 hours of a TAF; NWS **METARs** exclude trend forecasts. U.S. Military **TAFs** include Turbulence and Icing groups.

Aviation Routine Weather Report (METAR)

A METAR is an observation of current surface weather reported in a standard international format. METARs are issued on a regularly scheduled basis unless significant weather changes have occurred. A special METAR (SPECI) can be issued at any time between routine METAR reports. *Example:*

METAR KGGG 161753Z AUTO 14021G26KT 3/4SM +TSRA BR BKN008 OVC012CB 18/17 A2970 RMK PRESFR

A typical METAR report contains the following information in sequential order:

1. Type of report—there are two types of METAR reports. The first is the routine METAR report that is transmitted on a regular time interval. The second is the aviation selected SPECI. This is a special report that can be given at any time to update the METAR for rapidly changing weather conditions, aircraft mishaps, or other critical information.

2. Station identifier—a four-letter code as established by the International Civil Aviation Organization (ICAO). In the 48 contiguous states, a unique three-letter identifier is preceded by the letter "K." For example, Gregg County Airport in Longview, Texas, is identified by the letters "KGGG," K being the country designation and GGG being the airport identifier. In other regions of the world, including Alaska and Hawaii, the first two letters of the four-letter ICAO identifier indicate the region, country, or state. Alaska identifiers always begin with the letters "PA" and Hawaii identifiers always begin with the letters "PH." Station identifiers can be found by searching various websites such as DUATS and NOAA's Aviation Weather Aviation Digital Data Services (ADDS).

3. Date and time of report—depicted in a six-digit group (161753Z). The first two digits are the date. The last four digits are the time of the METAR/SPECI, which is always given in coordinated universal time (UTC). A "Z" is appended to the end of the time to denote the time is given in Zulu time (UTC) as opposed to local time.

4. Modifier—denotes that the METAR/SPECI came from an automated source or that the report was corrected. If the notation "AUTO" is listed in the METAR/SPECI, the report came from an automated source. It also lists "AO1" (for no precipitation discriminator) or "AO2" (with precipitation discriminator) in the "Remarks" section to indicate the type of precipitation sensors employed at the automated station. When the modifier "COR" is used, it identifies a corrected report sent out to replace an earlier report that contained an error (for example: METAR KGGG 161753Z COR).

5. Wind—reported with five digits (14021KT) unless the speed is greater than 99 knots, in which case the wind is reported with six digits. The first three digits indicate the direction the true wind is blowing from in tens of degrees. If the wind is variable, it is reported as "VRB." The last two digits indicate the speed of the wind in knots unless the wind is greater than 99 knots, in which case it is indicated by three digits. If the winds are gusting, the letter "G" follows the wind speed (G26KT). After the letter "G," the peak gust recorded is provided. If the wind direction varies more than 60° and the wind speed is greater than six knots, a separate group of numbers, separated by a "V," will indicate the extremes of the wind directions.

6. Visibility—the prevailing visibility (¾ SM) is reported in statute miles as denoted by the letters "SM." It is reported in both miles and fractions of miles. At times, runway visual range (RVR) is reported following the prevailing visibility. RVR is the distance a pilot can see down the runway in a moving aircraft. When RVR is reported, it is shown with an R, then the runway number followed by a slant, then the visual range in feet. For example, when the RVR is reported as R17L/1400FT, it translates to a visual range of 1,400 feet on runway 17 left.

7. Weather—can be broken down into two different categories: qualifiers and weather phenomenon (+TSRA BR). First, the qualifiers of intensity, proximity, and the descriptor of the weather are given. The intensity may be light (–), moderate ( ), or heavy (+). Proximity only depicts weather phenomena that

are in the airport vicinity. The notation "VC" indicates a specific weather phenomenon is in the vicinity of five to ten miles from the airport. Descriptors are used to describe certain types of precipitation and obscurations. Weather phenomena may be reported as being precipitation, obscurations, and other phenomena, such as squalls or funnel clouds. Descriptions of weather phenomena as they begin or end and hailstone size are also listed in the "Remarks" sections of the report. *See* Figure 3-5.

Qualifier				Weather Phenomena					
Intensity or Proximity 1		Descriptor 2		Precipitation 3		Obscuration 4		Other 5	
–	Light	MI	Shallow	DZ	Drizzle	BR	Mist	PO	Dust/sand whirls
	Moderate (no qualifier)	BC	Patches	RA	Rain	FG	Fog	SQ	Squalls
+	Heavy	DR	Low drifting	SN	Snow	FU	Smoke	FC	Funnel cloud
VC	in the vicinity	BL	Blowing	SG	Snow grains	DU	Dust	+FC	Tornado or waterspout
		SH	Showers	IC	Ice crystals (diamond dust)	SA	Sand	SS	Sandstorm
		TS	Thunderstorms	PL	Ice pellets	HZ	Haze	DS	Dust storm
		FZ	Freezing	GR	Hail	PY	Spray		
		PR	Partial	GS	Small hail or snow pellets	VA	Volcanic ash		
				UP	Unknown precipitation*				

The weather groups are constructed by considering columns 1–5 in this table in sequence: intensity, followed by descriptor, followed by weather phenomena (e.g., heavy rain shower(s) is coded as +SHRA).

Automated stations only.

Figure 3-5. Descriptors and weather phenomena used in a typical METAR

Sky Cover	Contraction
Less than 1/8 (Clear)	SKC, CLR, FEW
1/8–2/8 (Few)	FEW
3/8–4/8 (Scattered)	SCT
5/8–7/8 (Broken)	BKN
8/8 (Overcast)	OVC

Figure 3-6. Reportable contractions for sky condition

8. Sky condition—always reported in the sequence of amount, height, and type or indefinite ceiling/height (vertical visibility) (BKN008 OVC012CB, VV003). The heights of the cloud bases are reported with a three-digit number in hundreds of feet AGL. Clouds above 12,000 feet are not detected or reported by an automated station. The types of clouds, specifically towering cumulus (TCU) or cumulonimbus (CB) clouds, are reported with their height. Contractions are used to describe the amount of cloud coverage and obscuring phenomena. The amount of sky coverage is reported in eighths of the sky from horizon to horizon. *See* Figure 3-6.

9. Temperature and dew point—the air temperature and dew point are always given in degrees Celsius (C) or (18/17). Temperatures below 0 °C are preceded by the letter "M" to indicate minus.

10. Altimeter setting—reported as inches of mercury ("Hg) in a four-digit number group (A2970). It is always preceded by the letter "A." Rising or falling pressure may also be denoted in the "Remarks" sections as "PRESRR" or "PRESFR," respectively.

11. Zulu time—a term used in aviation for UTC, which places the entire world on one time standard.

12. Remarks—the remarks section always begins with the letters "RMK." Comments may or may not appear in this section of the METAR. The information contained in this section may include wind data, variable visibility, beginning and ending times of particular phenomenon, pressure information, and various other information deemed necessary. An example of a remark regarding weather phenomenon that does not fit in any other category would be: OCNL LTGICCG. This translates as occasional lightning in the clouds and from cloud to ground. Automated stations also use the remarks section to indicate the equipment needs maintenance.

Example:

METAR KGGG 161753Z AUTO 14021G26KT 3/4SM +TSRA BR BKN008 OVC012CB 18/17 A2970 RMK PRESFR

Explanation:

Routine METAR for Gregg County Airport for the 16th day of the month at 1753Z automated source. Winds are 140 at 21 knots gusting to 26. Visibility is ¾ statute mile. Thunderstorms with heavy rain and mist. Ceiling is broken at 800 feet, overcast at 1,200 feet with cumulonimbus clouds. Temperature 18 °C and dew point 17 °C. Barometric pressure is 29.70 "Hg and falling rapidly.

Aviation Forecasts

Observed weather condition reports are often used in the creation of forecasts for the same area. A variety of different forecast products are produced and designed to be used in the preflight planning stage. The printed forecasts that pilots need to be familiar with are the terminal aerodrome forecast (TAF), aviation area forecast (FA), inflight weather advisories (Significant Meteorological Information (SIGMET), Airman's Meteorological Information (AIRMET)), and the winds and temperatures aloft forecast (FB).

Terminal Aerodrome Forecasts (TAF)

A TAF is a report established for the five statute mile radius around an airport. TAF reports are usually given for larger airports. Each TAF is valid for a 24 or 30-hour time period and is updated four times a day at 0000Z, 0600Z, 1200Z, and 1800Z. The TAF utilizes the same descriptors and abbreviations as used in the METAR report. These weather reports can be beneficial to the remote pilot for flight planning purposes. The TAF includes the following information in sequential order:

1. Type of report—a TAF can be either a routine forecast (TAF) or an amended forecast (TAF AMD).

2. ICAO station identifier—the station identifier is the same as that used in a METAR.

3. Date and time of origin—time and date (081125Z) of TAF origination is given in the sixnumber code with the first two being the date, the last four being the time. Time is always given in UTC as denoted by the Z following the time block.

4. Valid period dates and times—The TAF valid period (0812/0912) follows the date/time of forecast origin group. Scheduled 24 and 30 hour TAFs are issued four times per day, at 0000, 0600, 1200, and 1800Z. The first two digits (08) are the day of the month for the start of the TAF. The next two digits (12) are the starting hour (UTC). 09 is the day of the month for the end of the TAF, and the last two digits (12) are the ending hour (UTC) of the valid period. A forecast period that begins at midnight UTC is annotated as 00. If the end time of a valid period is at midnight UTC, it is annotated as 24. For example, a 00Z TAF issued on the 9th of the month and valid for 24 hours would have a valid period of 0900/0924.

5. Forecast wind—the wind direction and speed forecast are coded in a five-digit number group. An example would be 15011KT. The first three digits indicate the direction of the wind in reference to true north. The last two digits state the wind speed in knots appended with "KT." Like the METAR, winds greater than 99 knots are given in three digits.

6. Forecast visibility—given in statute miles and may be in whole numbers or fractions. If the forecast is greater than six miles, it is coded as "P6SM."

7. Forecast significant weather—weather phenomena are coded in the TAF reports in the same format as the METAR.

8. Forecast sky condition—given in the same format as the METAR. Only CB clouds are forecast in this portion of the TAF report as opposed to CBs and towering cumulus in the METAR.

9. Forecast change group—for any significant weather change forecast to occur during the TAF time period, the expected conditions and time period are included in this group. This information may be shown as from (FM), and temporary (TEMPO). "FM" is used when a rapid and significant change,

usually within an hour, is expected. "TEMPO" is used for temporary fluctuations of weather, expected to last less than 1 hour.

10. PROB30—a given percentage that describes the probability of thunderstorms and precipitation occurring in the coming hours. This forecast is not used for the first 6 hours of the 24-hour forecast.

Example:

TAF KPIR 111130Z 1112/1212 TEMPO 1112/1114 5SM BR FM1500 16015G25KT P6SM SCT040 BKN250 FM120000 14012KT P6SM BKN080 OVC150 PROB30 1200/1204 3SM TSRA BKN030CB FM120400 1408KT P6SM SCT040 OVC080 TEMPO 1204/1208 3SM TSRA OVC030CB

Explanation:

Routine TAF for Pierre, South Dakota…on the 11th day of the month, at 1130Z…valid for 24 hours from 1200Z on the 11th to 1200Z on the 12th…wind from 150° at 12 knots… visibility greater than 6 SM…broken clouds at 9,000 feet… temporarily, between 1200Z and 1400Z, visibility 5 SM in mist… from 1500Z winds from 160° at 15 knots, gusting to 25 knots visibility greater than 6 SM…clouds scattered at 4,000 feet and broken at 25,000 feet…from 0000Z wind from 140° at 12 knots…visibility greater than 6 SM…clouds broken at 8,000 feet, overcast at 15,000 feet…between 0000Z and 0400Z, there is 30 percent probability of visibility 3 SM…thunderstorm with moderate rain showers… clouds broken at 3,000 feet with cumulonimbus clouds…from 0400Z…winds from 140° at 8 knots… visibility greater than 6 miles…clouds at 4,000 scattered and overcast at 8,000… temporarily between 0400Z and 0800Z…visibility 3 miles… thunderstorms with moderate rain showers…clouds overcast at 3,000 feet with cumulonimbus clouds…end of report (=).

Convective Significant Meteorological Information (WST)

Convective SIGMETs are issued for severe thunderstorms with surface winds greater than 50 knots, hail at the surface greater than or equal to ¾ inch in diameter, or tornadoes. They are also issued to advise pilots of embedded thunderstorms, lines of thunderstorms, or thunderstorms with heavy or greater precipitation that affect 40 percent or more of a 3,000 square mile or greater region. A remote pilot will find these weather alerts helpful for flight planning.

1179. Which statement is true concerning ASOS/AWOS weather reporting systems?

A— Each AWOS station is part of a nationwide network of weather reporting stations.
B— ASOS locations perform weather observing functions necessary to generate METAR reports.
C— Both ASOS and AWOS have the capability of reporting density altitude, as long as it exceeds the airport elevation by more than 1,000 feet.

ASOS is designed to support aviation operations and weather forecast activities. The ASOS will provide continuous minute-by-minute observations and perform the basic observing functions necessary to generate an aviation routine weather report (METAR) and other aviation weather information. (PLT514) — AIM ¶7-1-11

Answer (A) is incorrect because selected individual systems may be incorporated into nationwide data collection and dissemination networks. Answer (C) is incorrect because only the AWOS has the capability of reporting density altitude.

1180. (Refer to Figure 12.) The wind direction and velocity at KJFK is from:

A— 180° true at 4 knots.
B— 180° magnetic at 4 knots.
C— 040° true at 18 knots

The wind is reported as a five-digit group (six digits if speed is over 99 knots). The first three digits is the direction the wind is blowing from rounded to the nearest tens of degrees relative to true (not magnetic) north, or "VRB" if the direction is variable. The next two digits is the speed in knots, or if over 99 knots, the next three digits. If the wind is gusty, it is reported as a "G" after the speed followed by the highest gust reported. The abbreviation "KT" is appended to denote the use of knots for wind speed. The wind group for KJFK is 18004KT which means the wind is from 180° at 4 knots. (PLT059) — AC 00-45

Answers
1179 [B]   1180 [A]

1181. (Refer to Figure 12.) What are the current conditions for Chicago Midway Airport (KMDW)?

A— Sky 700 feet overcast, visibility 1-1/2 SM, rain.
B— Sky 7,000 feet overcast, visibility 1-1/2 SM, heavy rain.
C— Sky 700 feet overcast, visibility 11, occasionally 2 SM, with rain.

The current conditions at KMDW are 1-1/2 SM visibility (1-1/2 SM) with rain (RA), ceiling overcast at 700 feet (OVC007). (PLT059) — AC 00-45

1182. (Refer to Figure 15.) In the TAF for KMEM, what does "SHRA" stand for?

A— Rain showers.
B— A shift in wind direction is expected.
C— A significant change in precipitation is possible.

"SH" stands for showers, and "RA" stands for rain. (PLT072) — AC 00-45

Answers (B) and (C) are incorrect because a permanent change in existing conditions during the valid period of the TAF is indicated by the change groups FMHH (FroM) and BECMG (BECoMinG) HHhh.

1183. (Refer to Figure 15.) Between 1000Z and 1200Z the visibility at KMEM is forecast to be

A— 1/2 statute mile.
B— 3 statute miles.
C— 6 statute miles.

Between 1000Z and 1200Z, the visibility at KMEM is forecast to be 3 statute miles (BECMG 1012...3SM). (PLT072) — AC 00-45

1184. (Refer to Figure 15.) What is the forecast wind for KMEM from 1600Z until the end of the forecast?

A— No significant wind.
B— Variable in direction at 4 knots.
C— Variable in direction at 6 knots.

From 1600Z until the end of the forecast, wind will be variable in direction at 6 knots (VRB06KT). (PLT072) — AC 00-45

1185. (Refer to Figure 15.) According to the KMEM forecast, what is the earliest time on the 12th (today) at which the visibility may be reduced below the 3 SM minimum for sUAS operations?

A— 1720Z
B— 2200Z
C— 2000Z

Between 2000Z and 2200Z there is a 40% probability (PROB) that the visibility will drop to 1 SM due to a thunderstorm (TS) and moderate rain (RA). (PLT072) — AC 00-45

1311. What will a convective SIGMET be issued for?

A— Squall line thunderstorms.
B— Visibility less than 3 miles.
C— Surface winds greater than 40 knots.

Any convective SIGMET implies severe or greater turbulence, severe icing, and low-level wind shear. The forecast may be issued for any of the following—severe thunderstorms due to:

1. *Surface winds greater than or equal to 50 knots, or*

2. *Hail at the surface greater than or equal to 3/4 inch in diameter, or*

3. *Tornadoes, embedded thunderstorms, lines of thunderstorms.*

(PLT290) — AC 00-45

1292. (Refer to Figure 12.) The remarks section for KMDW has "RAB35" listed. This entry means

A— blowing mist has reduced the visibility to 1-1/2 SM.
B— rain began at 1835Z.
C— the barometer has risen .35" Hg.

The entry RAB35 means that rain began 35 minutes past the hour. (PLT059) — AC 00-45

Answer (A) is incorrect because mist is reported as BR. Answer (C) is incorrect because there is no format for reporting an altimeter change in a METAR.

Answers

1181 [A]   1182 [A]   1183 [B]   1184 [C]   1185 [C]   1311 [A]
1292 [B]

Chapter 4
Loading and Performance

Introduction

The remote pilot-in-command is responsible for ensuring the sUAS is in a condition for safe operation. Part of this involves checking for proper loading, so that the device operates to the expected performance standards.

Prior to each flight, the remote PIC must ensure that any object attached to or carried by the small unmanned aircraft is secure and does not adversely affect the flight characteristics or controllability of the aircraft. For example, some small UA do not have a set holder or slot for the battery; instead, it is simply attached with hook-and-loop or other type of fastener. This allows some leeway on the lateral and longitudinal location of the battery on the small UA. Remote pilots should ensure the battery is installed in the proper location so it does not adversely affect the controllability of the aircraft. The attachments must be secure so the battery does not move during flight. Similar concerns exist and cautions advised if any external attachments are installed. Also be sure to close and lock (if applicable) all panels or doors.

Follow all manufacturer recommendations for evaluating performance to ensure safe and efficient operation. This manufacturer information may include operational performance details for the aircraft such as launch, climb, range, endurance, descent, and landing. It is important to understand the significance of the operational data to be able to make practical use of the aircraft's capabilities and limitations. The manufacturers' information regarding performance data is not standardized; availability and how this information is conveyed can vary greatly between sUAS types. If manufacturer-published performance data is unavailable, the remote pilot should seek out performance data that may have already been determined and published by other users of the same sUAS manufacturer model, and use that data as a starting point.

Check weather conditions prior to and during every sUAS flight and consider the effects of weather on aircraft performance.

Airplane flight control systems consist of primary and secondary systems. The ailerons, elevator (or stabilator) and rudder constitute the primary control system and are required to control an airplane safely during flight. Wing flaps, leading edge devices, spoilers and trim systems constitute the secondary control system and improve the performance characteristics of the airplane or relieve the pilot of excessive control forces. *See* Figure 4-1.

A helicopter has four flight control inputs: cyclic, collective, antitorque pedals, and throttle. The cyclic can vary the pitch of the rotor blades throughout each revolution of the main rotor system to develop lift (thrust). The result is to tilt the rotor disk in a particular direction, resulting in the helicopter moving in that direction.

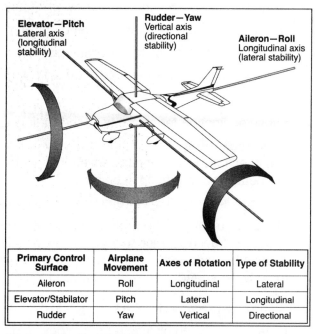

Primary Control Surface	Airplane Movement	Axes of Rotation	Type of Stability
Aileron	Roll	Longitudinal	Lateral
Elevator/Stabilator	Pitch	Lateral	Longitudinal
Rudder	Yaw	Vertical	Directional

Figure 4-1. Aircraft flight controls

1186. Before each flight, the remote PIC must ensure that

A— ATC has granted clearance.
B— the site supervisor has approved the flight.
C— objects carried on the sUAS are secure.

Prior to each flight, the remote PIC must ensure that any object attached to or carried by the small unmanned aircraft is secure and does not adversely affect the flight characteristics or controllability of the aircraft. (PLT445) — AC 107-2

Answers

1186 [C]

1300. What purpose does a rudder perform on an sUAS airplane?

A— The rudder controls yaw.
B— The rudder controls bank.
C— The rudder controls pitch.

The purpose of the rudder is to control yaw. (PLT026) — FAA-H-8083-25

Answer (B) is incorrect because the ailerons control bank. Answer (C) is incorrect because pitch is controlled by the elevator.

Determining Speed and Altitude

The remote pilot must not exceed these regulatory limitations for operating an sUAS:

- Cannot be flown faster than a ground speed of 87 knots (100 miles per hour).

- Cannot be flown higher than 400 feet above ground level (AGL) unless flown within a 400-foot radius of a structure and is not flown higher than 400 feet above the structure's immediate uppermost limit.

Some of the possible ways to ensure that 87 knots is not exceeded include:

- Installing a Global Positioning System (GPS) device on the sUAS that reports ground speed information to the remote pilot, wherein the remote pilot takes into account the wind direction and speed and calculates the sUAS airspeed for a given direction of flight;

- Timing the ground speed of the sUAS when it is flown between two or more fixed points, taking into account wind speed and direction between each point, then noting the power settings of the sUAS to operate at or less than 87 knots ground speed;

- Using the sUAS's manufacturer design limitations (e.g., installed ground speed limiters);

- Using a radar gun to measure speed of the sUAS;

- Using an anemometer coupled with inertial information from onboard sensors; or

- Using inertial sensors capable of detecting wind speed and velocity as well as sUAS movement to determine ground speed.

These navigation terms are used in aviation as related to ground speed:

- **Dead reckoning** is navigation solely by means of computations based on time, airspeed, distance, and direction. The products derived from these variables, when adjusted by windspeed and velocity, are heading and ground speed.

- **Pilotage** is navigation by reference to landmarks or checkpoints.

- The **wind triangle** is navigation using triangulation. The true heading and the ground speed can be found by drawing a wind triangle of vectors. One side of the triangle is the wind direction and velocity; another side is the true heading and true airspeed, the last side is the track, or true course, and the ground speed. Each side of a wind triangle is the vector sum of the other two sides.

Some possible ways for a remote pilot to determine altitude above the ground or structure are as follows:

- Install a calibrated altitude reporting device on the sUAS that reports the sUAS altitude above mean sea level (MSL) to the remote pilot, wherein the remote pilot subtracts the MSL elevation of the control station from the sUAS-reported MSL altitude to determine the sUAS altitude above the terrain or structure.

- Install a GPS device on the sUAS that also has the capability of reporting MSL altitude to the remote pilot (note that there may be minor errors associated with using this type of altitude reporting).

Answers

1300 [A]

- With the sUAS on the ground, have the remote pilot and VO pace off 400 feet from the sUAS to get a visual perspective of the sUAS at that distance, wherein the remote pilot and VO maintain that visual perspective or closer while the sUAS is in flight.
- Use the known height of local rising terrain and/or structures as a reference.
- If the control station has a measure of distance between it and the UA, fly directly overhead until reaching 400 feet and note the visual perspective.

In addition to local resources, the sectional chart for that region should be consulted for information on the altitude of the terrain and structures. Towers and other known obstructions are depicted with their altitude noted. It is critical to understand that altitude dimensions of airspace depicted on sectional charts are in MSL; remote pilots must be careful to properly convert between AGL and MSL as applicable to their equipment, operation, and regulation restrictions. *See* Legend 1 in the CT-8080-2X.

1187. You are operating an sUAS that does not have GPS or an installed ground speed limiter. How can you determine the speed you are operating?

A— Dead reckoning.
B— Pilotage.
C— Wind triangle.

Without a GPS or manufacturer performance data, you can determine speed by timing the ground speed of the sUAS when it is flown between two or more fixed points, taking into account wind speed and direction between each point, then noting the power settings of the sUAS to operate at or less than 87 knots ground speed. This is a form of dead reckoning. (PLT200) — FAA-H-8083-25, AC 107-2

Answer (B) is incorrect because pilotage will help with navigating the sectional chart but cannot be used to determine ground speed. Answer (C) is incorrect because the wind triangle requires that you know true airspeed to determine ground speed; without instrumentation installed on the sUAS you won't have that information.

1188. How can a remote pilot determine the altitude of the terrain and structures where the flight will be conducted?

A— Sectional Chart.
B— Manufacturers data.
C— Road maps.

Refer to Legend 1. In addition to local resources, the sectional chart for that region should be consulted for information on the altitude of the terrain and structures. Towers and other known obstructions are depicted with their altitude noted. (PLT064) — Sectional Chart

1189. You are operating an sUAS that does not have GPS or an installed altimeter. How can you determine the altitude you are operating?

A— Gaining a visual perspective of what 400 feet looks like on the ground before the flight.
B— Operating a second sUAS that has an altimeter to gain a visual perspective of 400 feet from the air.
C— Operating the sUAS in close proximity of a tower known to be 400 feet tall.

To determine altitude, with the sUAS on the ground, the remote pilot and VO should pace off 400 feet from the sUAS to get a visual perspective of the sUAS at that distance, wherein the remote pilot and VO maintain that visual perspective or closer while the sUAS is in flight. (PLT43) — AC 107-2

Answer (B) is incorrect because a person may not operate or act as a remote PIC or VO in the operation of more than one UA at the same time. Answer (C) is incorrect because the remote PIC needs to adhere to wire strike avoidance procedures when operating near towers, which are likely to have guy wires.

Loading

As with any aircraft, compliance with weight and balance limits is critical to the safety of flight for sUAS. An unmanned aircraft that is loaded out of balance may exhibit unexpected and unsafe flight characteristics. An overweight condition may cause problematic control or performance limitations. Before any flight, verify that the unmanned aircraft is correctly loaded by determining the weight and balance condition.

Continued

Answers
1187 [A]   1188 [A]   1189 [A]

- Review any available manufacturer weight and balance data and follow all restrictions and limitations.

- If the manufacturer does not provide specific weight and balance data, apply general weight and balance principals to determine limits for a given flight. For example, add weight to the unmanned aircraft in a manner that does not adversely affect the aircraft's **center of gravity (CG)** location—a point at which the unmanned aircraft would balance if it were suspended at that point. Usually this is located near the geographical center of multi-copters but may vary along the centerline of the fuselage of fixed-wing and single-rotor UA.

Although a maximum gross launch weight may be specified, the aircraft may not always safely take off with this load under all conditions. Or if it does become airborne, the unmanned aircraft may exhibit unexpected and unusually poor flight characteristics. Conditions that affect launch and climb performance, such as high elevations, high air temperatures, and high humidity (high density altitudes) as well as windy conditions may require a reduction in weight before flight is attempted. Other factors to consider prior to launch are runway/launch area length, surface, slope, surface wind, and the presence of obstacles. These factors may require a reduction in weight prior to flight.

Weight changes during flight also have a direct effect on aircraft performance. Fuel burn is the most common weight change that takes place during flight. As fuel is used, the aircraft becomes lighter and performance is improved, but this could have a negative effect on balance. For battery-powered sUAS operations, weight change during flight may occur when expendable items are used on board (e.g., a jettisonable load such as an agricultural spray). Changes of mounted equipment between flights, such as the installation of different cameras, battery packs, or other instruments, may also affect the weight and balance and performance of an sUAS.

Adverse balance conditions (i.e., weight distribution) may affect flight characteristics in much the same manner as an excess weight condition. Limits for the location of the CG may be established by the manufacturer and may be covered in the Pilot Operating Handbook (POH) or UAS flight manual. The CG is not a fixed point marked on the aircraft; its location depends on the distribution of aircraft weight. As variable load items are shifted or expended, there may be a resultant shift in CG location. The remote PIC should determine how the CG will shift and the resultant effects on the aircraft. If the CG is not within the allowable limits after loading or do not remain within the allowable limits for safe flight, it will be necessary to relocate or shed some weight before flight is attempted.

Excessive weight reduces the flight performance in almost every respect. In addition, operating above the maximum weight limitation can compromise the structural integrity of an unmanned aircraft. The most common performance deficiencies of an overloaded aircraft are:

- Reduced rate of climb,
- Lower maximum altitude,
- Shorter endurance, and
- Reduced maneuverability.

Prior to conducting a mission or extended flight, it is recommended to test-fly the UA to determine if there are any unexpected performance issues due to loading. This testing should be done away from obstacles and people.

Computing Weight and Balance

The **empty weight** is obtained from manufacturers' documentation. It includes the airframe, power source, all fixed equipment, and unusable fuel. The **useful load** includes the power source (battery or fuel) and payload or mission equipment (such as a camera). The launch weight is the empty weight plus the useful load. The landing weight is the launch weight minus any fuel used or jettisoned load.

The **arm** is the horizontal distance measured in inches from the datum line (a reference point along the longitudinal axis indicated by the manufacturer) to a point on the sUAS. If measured aft, toward the defined rear of the aircraft, the arm is given a positive (+) value; if measured forward, toward the defined front, the arm is given a negative (-) value.

The **moment** is the product of the weight of an object multiplied by its arm and is expressed in pound-inches (lbs-in). The moment is essentially a force being applied at a location along the longitudinal axis, which must be countered by the control capabilities of the aircraft. If moment(s) exceed the control capacity of the aircraft, it becomes unstable or uncontrollable. The formula that is used to find moment is usually expressed as follows: Weight × Arm = Moment.

The CG is the point about which an aircraft will balance, and it is expressed in inches from datum. The CG is found by dividing the total moment by the total weight, and the formula is usually expressed as follows: Total Moment = CG (inches aft of datum) / Total Weight.

Lateral center of gravity is also important (measured along the horizontal axis). Uneven distribution of weight on one side of the aircraft versus the other may cause controllability and/or performance issues.

1190. When loading cameras or other equipment on an sUAS, mount the items in a manner that

A— is visible to the visual observer or other crewmembers.
B— does not adversely affect the center of gravity.
C— can be easily removed without the use of tools.

Any mounted equipment should be balanced in a manner that does not adversely affect the center of gravity or result in unsafe performance. (PLT313) — AC 107-2

1191. To ensure that the unmanned aircraft center of gravity (CG) limits are not exceeded, follow the aircraft loading instructions specified in the

A— Aircraft Weight and Balance Handbook.
B— Pilot's Operating Handbook or UAS Flight Manual.
C— Aeronautical Information Manual (AIM).

Before any flight, verify that the unmanned aircraft is correctly loaded by determining the weight and balance condition. Review any available manufacturer weight and balance data and follow all restrictions and limitations. (PLT313) — FAA-H-8083-1

1192. What could be a consequence of operating a small unmanned aircraft above its maximum allowable weight?

A— Shorter endurance.
B— Increased maneuverability.
C— Faster speed.

Excessive weight reduces the flight performance in almost every respect, including a shorter endurance. In addition, operating above the maximum weight limitation can compromise the structural integrity of an unmanned aircraft. (PLT313) — AC 107-2

1193. When operating an aircraft, the Remote PIC is responsible for using

A— the most current weight and balance data.
B— weight and balance data from the factory.
C— recent weight and balance data.

It is the responsibility of the remote PIC to use the most current weight and balance data when planning a flight and operating the sUAS. (PLT242) — FAA-H-8083-1

1194. Which of the following is true regarding weight and balance of small unmanned aircraft?

A— CG cannot change during flight.
B— Lateral CG is not important to small unmanned aircraft operations.
C— Operations outside weight and balance limitations may result in loss of control.

Loading the aircraft outside of limitations (weight, balance, or both) may lead to moments that exceed the capabilities of the flight controls/engine(s), thus possibly leading to loss of control or other performance anomalies. (PLT242) — FAA-H8083-1

Answers

1190 [B]	1191 [B]	1192 [A]	1193 [A]	1194 [C]

1293. A UAS loaded with the most rearward center of gravity is

A— less stable at all speeds.
B— more stable at slow speeds.
C— more stable at fast speeds.

Operation with the center of gravity (CG) outside the approved limits results in control difficulty. (PLT312) — FAA-H-8083-25

Load Factor

In aerodynamics, **load** is the force or imposed stress that must be supported by an sUAS structure in flight. The loads imposed on the wings or rotors in flight are stated in terms of **load factor**. In straight-and-level flight, the sUAS wings/rotors support a load equal to the sum of the weight of the sUAS plus its contents. This particular load factor is equal to "One G," where "**G**" refers to the pull of gravity. However, centrifugal force is generated which acts toward the outside of the curve any time an sUAS is flying a curved path (turns, climbs, or descents).

Angle of bank	Load factor
0°	1.000
10°	1.015
30°	1.154
45°	1.414
60°	2.000
70°	2.923
80°	5.747
85°	11.473
90°	∞

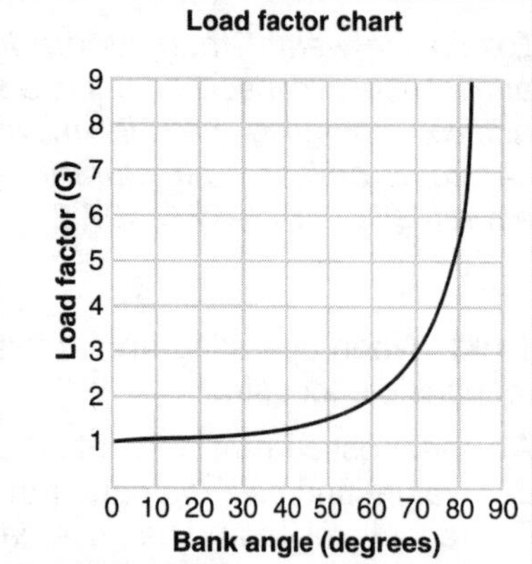

Load factor chart

Figure 4-2. Load factor chart

Unmanned aircraft performance can be decreased due to an increase in load factor when the aircraft is operated in maneuvers other than straight and level flight. The load factor increases at a significant rate after a bank (turn) has reached 45° or 50°. The load factor for any aircraft in a coordinated level turn at 60° bank is 2 Gs. The load factor in an 80° bank is 5.75 Gs. *See* Figure 4-2. The wing must produce lift equal to these load factors if altitude is to be maintained. The remote PIC should be mindful of the increased load factor and its possible effects on the aircraft's structural integrity and the results of an increase in stall speed. These principles apply to both fixed wing and rotor wing designs, but in the case of rotor wing type unmanned aircraft, the weight/load must be supported by the lift generated by the propellers.

As with manned aircraft, an unmanned aircraft will stall when critical angle of attack of the wing or rotors/propeller is exceeded. This can occur when an unmanned aircraft is turned too sharply/tightly or pitched up too steeply or rapidly. Remote pilots of rotor type unmanned aircraft should use particular caution when descending in a vertical straight line. In some cases, the turbulent downward airflow can disrupt the normal production of lift by the propellers as well as cause problematic air circulation producing vortices. These phenomena are referred to as vortex ring state or settling with power, and when they occur the aircraft can wobble, descend rapidly, or become uncontrollable. Recovery from this state of flight requires forward or rearward motion—counterintuitively, the addition of power to arrest the descent only makes the situation worse. Due to the low-altitude operating environment, consideration should be given to ensure aircraft control is maintained and the aircraft is not operated outside its performance limits.

Answers

1293 [A]

1195. When operating an unmanned aircraft, the remote pilot-in-command should consider that the load factor on the wings or rotors may be increased anytime

A— the aircraft is subjected to maneuvers other than straight and level flight.
B— the CG is shifted rearward to the aft CG limit.
C— the gross weight is reduced.

Unmanned airplane performance can be decreased due to an increase in load factor when the airplane is operated in maneuvers other than straight and level flight. (PLT310) — FAA-H-8083-25

1196. (Refer to Figure 2.) If an sUAS weighs 10 pounds, what approximate weight would the sUAS structure be required to support during a 60° banked turn while maintaining altitude?

A— 10.15 pounds.
B— 30 pounds.
C— 20 pounds.

Refer to Figure 2 and use the following steps:

1. Enter the chart at a 60° angle of bank and proceed upward to the curved reference line. From the point of intersection, move to the left side of the chart and read a load factor of 2 Gs.

2. Multiply the aircraft weight by the load factor: 10 x 2 = 20 lbs. Or, working from the table: 10 x 2.0 (load factor) = 20 lbs.

(PLT018) — FAA-H-8083-25

1197. (Refer to Figure 2.) If an sUAS weighs 50 pounds, what approximate weight would the sUAS structure be required to support during a 30° banked turn while maintaining altitude?

A— 60 pounds.
B— 45 pounds.
C— 30 pounds.

Referencing Figure 2, use the following steps:

1. Enter the chart at a 30° angle of bank and proceed upward to the curved reference line. From the point of intersection, move to the left side of the chart and read an approximate load factor of 1.2 Gs.

2. Multiply the aircraft weight by the load factor: 50 × 1.2 = 60 lbs. Or, working from the table: 50 1.154 (load factor) = 57.7 lbs.

(PLT018) — FAA-H-8083-25

Answers (B) and (C) are incorrect because they are less than 50 pounds; load factor increases with bank for level flight.

1198. (Refer to Figure 2.) If an unmanned airplane weighs 33 pounds, what approximate weight would the airplane structure be required to support during a 30° banked turn while maintaining altitude?

A— 34 pounds.
B— 47 pounds.
C— 38 pounds.

Referencing Figure 2, use the following steps:

1. Enter the chart at a 30° angle of bank and proceed upward to the curved reference line. From the point of intersection, move to the left side of the chart and read an approximate load factor of 1.2 Gs.

2. Multiply the aircraft weight by the load factor: 33 × 1.2 = 39.6 lbs. Or, working from the table: 33 × 1.154 (load factor) = 38.1 lbs.

(PLT018) — FAA-H-8083-25

1199. The amount of excess load that can be imposed on the wing of an airplane depends upon the

A— position of the CG.
B— speed of the airplane.
C— abruptness at which the load is applied.

At slow speeds, the maximum available lifting force of the wing is only slightly greater than the amount necessary to support the weight of the sUAS. However, at high speeds, the capacity of the flight controls, or a strong gust, may increase the load factor beyond safe limits. (PLT310) — FAA-H-8083-25

Answer (A) is incorrect because the position of the CG affects the stability of the sUAS, but not the total load the wings can support. Answer (C) is incorrect because abrupt control inputs do not limit load.

Answers

1195 [A]	1196 [C]	1197 [A]	1198 [C]	1199 [B]

1200. Which basic flight maneuver increases the load factor on an sUAS as compared to straight-and-level flight?

A— Climbs.
B— Turns.
C— Stalls.

A change in speed during straight flight will not produce any appreciable change in load, but when a change is made in the sUAS flight path, an additional load is imposed upon the structure. This is particularly true if a change in direction is made at high speeds with rapid, forceful control movements. (PLT310) — FAA-H-8083-25

Answer (A) is incorrect because the load increases only as the angle of attack is changed, momentarily. Once the climb attitude has been set, the wings only carry the load produced by the weight of the aircraft. Answer (C) is incorrect because in a stall, the wings are not producing lift.

Stalls

An **airfoil** is a structure or body that produces a useful reaction to air movement. Airplane wings, helicopter rotor blades, and propellers are airfoils. The **chord line** is an imaginary straight line from the leading edge to the trailing edge of an airfoil. In aerodynamics, **relative wind** is the wind "felt" or experienced by an airfoil. It is created by the movement of air past an airfoil, by the motion of an airfoil through the air, or by a combination of the two. Relative wind is parallel to, and in the opposite direction of the flight path of the airfoil. The **angle of attack** is the angle between the chord line of the airfoil and the relative wind. Angle of attack is directly related to the generation of lift by an airfoil. *See* Figures 4-3 through 4-6.

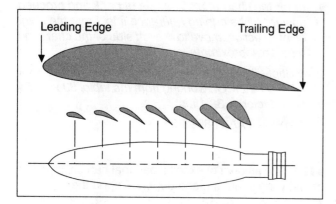

Figure 4-3. A typical airfoil cross-section

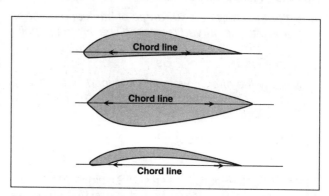

Figure 4-4. Chord line

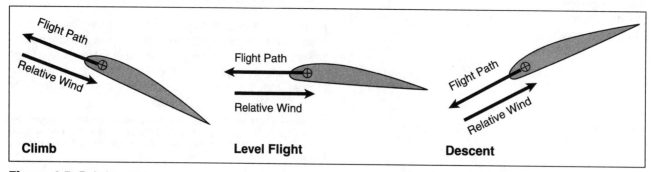

Figure 4-5. Relative wind

Answers

1200 [B]

As the angle of attack is increased (to increase lift), the air will no longer flow smoothly over the upper airfoil surface but instead will become turbulent or "burble" near the trailing edge. A further increase in the angle of attack will cause the turbulent area to expand forward. At an angle of attack of approximately 18° to 20° (for most airfoils), turbulence over the upper wing surface decreases lift so drastically that flight cannot be sustained and the airfoil "stalls." *See* Figure 4-7. The angle at which a stall occurs is called the **critical angle of attack**. An unmanned aircraft can stall at any airspeed or any attitude, but will always stall at the same critical angle of attack. The critical angle of attack of an airfoil is a function of its design therefore does not change based upon weight, maneuvering, or density altitude. However, the airspeed (strength of the relative wind) at which a given aircraft will stall in a particular configuration will remain the same regardless of altitude.

Because air density decreases with an increase in altitude, an unmanned aircraft must have greater forward speed to encounter the same strength of relative wind as would be experienced with the thicker air at lower altitudes. An easier way to envision this concept is to imagine how many molecules of air pass over an airfoil per second—thicker air at lower altitudes has more air molecules for a given area than the thinner air at higher altitudes. In order to successfully keep an aircraft aloft, a minimum number of air molecules must pass over the airfoil per second. As fewer molecules are available to make the journey as altitude increases, the only way to ensure that the aircraft can stay aloft is to increase its forward speed, thus forcing more air molecules over the airfoil each second.

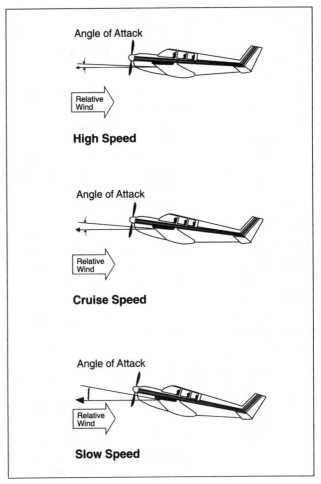

Figure 4-6. Angle of attack

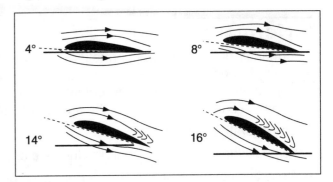

Figure 4-7. Flow of air over wing at various angles of attack

1201. The term "angle of attack" is defined as the angle

A— between the wing chord line and the relative wind.
B— between the airplane's climb angle and the horizon.
C— formed by the longitudinal axis of the airplane and the chord line of the wing.

The angle of attack is the acute angle between the relative wind and the chord line of the wing. (PLT168) — FAA-H-8083-25

Answer (B) is incorrect because there is no specific aviation term for this. Answer (C) is incorrect because this is the definition of the angle of incidence.

Answers
1201 [A]

1202. The angle of attack at which an airfoil stalls will

A— increase if the CG is moved forward.
B— remain the same regardless of gross weight.
C— change with an increase in gross weight.

When the angle of attack is increased to between 18° and 20° (critical angle of attack) on most airfoils, the airstream can no longer follow the upper curvature of the wing because of the excessive change in direction. The airfoil will stall if the critical angle of attack is exceeded. The airspeed at which stall occurs will be determined by weight and load factor, but the stall angle of attack is the same. (PLT168) — FAA-H-8083-25

1203. A stall occurs when the smooth airflow over the unmanned aircraft's wing/propeller(s) is disrupted, and the lift reduces rapidly. This is caused when the wing/propeller(s)

A— exceeds maximum allowable operating weight.
B— exceeds the maximum speed.
C— exceeds its critical angle of attack.

The airfoil will stall if the critical angle of attack is exceeded. (PLT312) — FAA-H-8083-3

Answer (A) is incorrect because while exceeding the maximum allowable operating weight could compromise the structural integrity and decrease controllability, it does not necessarily result in a stall. Answer (B) is incorrect because while the remote pilot may not fly faster than 87 knots (100 mph) or the manufacturer recommended maximum speed, exceeding these do not necessarily result in a stall.

1204. An increase in load factor will cause an unmanned aircraft to

A— stall at a higher airspeed.
B— have a tendency to spin.
C— be more difficult to control.

Stall speed increases in proportion to the square root of the load factor. Thus, with a load factor of 4, an aircraft will stall at a speed which is double the normal stall speed. (PLT310) — FAA-H-8083-25

Answer (B) is incorrect because an airplane's tendency to spin does not relate to an increase in load factors. Answer (C) is incorrect because an airplane's stability determines its controllability.

1314. In a 45° banking turn, a UA will

A— be more susceptible to spinning.
B— stall at a higher airspeed.
C— stall at a lower airspeed.

Stall speed increases in proportion to the square root of the load factor. Thus, with a load factor of 4, an aircraft will stall at a speed which is double the normal stall speed. (PLT328) — FAA-H-8083-25

Performance

Performance or operational information may be provided by the manufacturer in the form of Pilot's Operating Handbook, owner's manual, or on the manufacturer's website. Follow all manufacturer recommendations for evaluating performance to ensure safe and efficient operation. Even when specific performance data is not provided, the remote PIC should be familiar with:

- The operating environment.

- All available information regarding the safe and recommended operation of the sUAS.

- Conditions that may impact the performance or controllability of the sUAS.

Even when operational data is not supplied by the manufacturer, the remote PIC can better understand the unmanned aircraft's capabilities and limitations by establishing a process for tracking malfunctions, defects, and flight characteristics in various environments and conditions. Use this operational data to establish a baseline for determining performance, reliability, and risk assessment for your particular system.

The remote PIC is responsible for ensuring that every flight can be accomplished safely, does not pose an undue hazard, and does not increase the likelihood of a loss of positive control. Consider how your decisions affect the safety of flight. For example:

Answers

1202 [B]   1203 [C]   1204 [A]   1314 [B]

- If you attempt flight in windy conditions, the unmanned aircraft may require an unusually high power setting to maneuver. This action may cause a rapid depletion of battery power and result in a failure mode.

- If you attempt flight in wintery weather conditions, ice may accumulate on the unmanned aircraft's surface. Ice increases the weight and adversely affects performance characteristics of the small unmanned aircraft.

Due to the diversity and rapidly-evolving nature of sUAS operations, individual remote PICs have flexibility to determine what equipage methods, if any, mitigate risk sufficiently to meet performance-based requirements, such as the prohibition against creating an undue hazard if there is a loss of aircraft control.

1205. According to 14 CFR Part 107, who is responsible for determining the performance of a small unmanned aircraft?

A— Remote pilot-in-command.
B— Manufacturer.
C— Owner or operator.

The remote PIC is responsible for ensuring that every flight can be accomplished safely, does not pose an undue hazard, and does not increase the likelihood of a loss of positive control. (PLT454) — 14 CFR §107.12

1206. What effect does an uphill terrain slope have on launch performance?

A— Increases launch speed.
B— Increases launch distance.
C— Decreases launch distance.

The effect of runway slope on launch distance is due to the component of weight along the inclined path of the aircraft. An upslope would contribute a retarding force component, while a downslope would contribute an accelerating force component. In the case of an upslope, the retarding force component adds to drag and rolling friction to reduce the net accelerating force. (PLT129) — FAA-H-8083-25

Answer (A) is incorrect because runway slope has no effect on the launch speed. Answer (C) is incorrect because an upslope will increase the launch distance required.

1207. The most critical conditions of launch performance are the result of some combination of high gross weight, altitude, temperature, and

A— unfavorable wind.
B— obstacles surrounding the launch site.
C— powerplant systems.

The most critical conditions of launch performance are the result of some combination of high gross weight, altitude, temperature, and unfavorable wind. In all cases, the remote pilot must make an accurate prediction of takeoff distance from the performance data of the AFM/POH, regardless of the runway available, and strive for polished, professional launch procedures. (PLT134) — FAA-H-8083-25

1208. Maximum endurance is obtained at the point of minimum power to maintain the aircraft

A— in steady, level flight.
B— in a long range descent.
C— at its slowest possible indicated airspeed.

The maximum endurance condition is obtained at the point of minimum power required since this would require the lowest fuel flow or battery to keep the sUAS in steady, level flight. Maximum range condition occurs where the proportion between speed and power required is greatest. (PLT015) — FAA-H-8083-25

Answers
1205 [A]　　　1206 [B]　　　1207 [A]　　　1208 [A]

1209. When range and economy of operation are the principle goals, the remote pilot must ensure that the sUAS will be operated at the recommended

A— specific endurance.
B— long-range cruise performance.
C— equivalent airspeed.

Total range is dependent on both fuel available and specific range. When range and economy of operation are the principle goals, the remote pilot must ensure that the sUAS is operated at the recommended long-range cruise condition. By this procedure, the sUAS will be capable of its maximum design-operating radius, or can achieve lesser flight distances with a maximum of fuel reserve at the destination. (PLT130) — FAA-H-8083-25

1210. What is the best source for sUAS performance data and information?

A— Manufacturer publications.
B— Pilot reports.
C— Estimates based upon similar systems.

The manufacturer is the best source of performance data and information, if available. (PLT122) — FAA-H-8083-25

Chapter 5
Operations

Introduction

Before each flight, the remote PIC must perform tasks to ensure that the sUAS is in a condition for safe operation. This preflight inspection should be conducted in accordance with the sUAS manufacturer's inspection procedures when available (usually found in the manufacturer's owner or maintenance manual) and/or an inspection procedure developed by the sUAS owner or operator.

Such inspections should focus on evaluating equipment for damage or other malfunction(s). The preflight check should be performed prior to each flight and include an appropriate UAS preflight inspection that is specific and scalable to the UAS, the program, and the operation. This should encompass the entire system in order to determine a continual condition for safe operation prior to flight. If manufacturers do not provide a preflight checklist or guide, Remote PICs should create their own guidelines to properly check all components critical to the safety and operation of flight.

An example of a common issue with sUAS is propeller damage or installation issues. Propeller blades can have nicks, cracks, bends, etc. that significantly degrade the structural integrity of the blade and could potentially impact the controllability and overall safety of the sUAS. Also, propeller installation must be done per the manufacturer guidelines. Failure to do so can lead to separation of the blade inflight, loss of control, damage to the sUAS, and/or injury to the user or other persons in the area.

Another important item to consider during the preflight inspection is the security of panels, doors, and other components as well as the security of attachments of object such as the camera, antennae, and the battery. Batteries should be inspected for damage or malfunctions. If a battery is "bloated" or looks abnormal in anyway, it should not be used or charged. A good practice is to turn on the engine(s)/motor(s) to ensure they are working properly followed by a brief, low altitude "test flight" to verify controllability, radio link, and system integrity.

At minimum, the preflight inspection should include a visual or functional check of the following items:

1. Visual condition inspection of the UAS components.
2. Airframe structure (including undercarriage), all flight control surfaces, and linkages.
3. Registration markings, for proper display and legibility.
4. Moveable control surfaces, including airframe attachment points.
5. Servo motor(s), including attachment point(s).
6. Propulsion system, including powerplants, propellers, rotors, ducted fans, etc.
7. Verify all systems (e.g., aircraft and control unit) have an adequate energy (fuel/battery) supply for the intended operation and are functioning properly.
8. Avionics, including control link transceiver, communication/navigation equipment, and antennas.
9. Calibrate UAS compass prior to all flights.
10. Control link transceiver, communication/navigation data link transceiver, and antennas.
11. Display panel, if used, is functioning properly.
12. Ground support equipment, including takeoff and landing systems, for proper operation.
13. Control link correct functionality is established between the aircraft and the CS.
14. Correct movement of control surfaces using the CS.
15. Onboard navigation and communication data links.
16. Flight termination system, if installed.
17. Fuel, for correct type and quantity; and/or
18. Battery levels for the aircraft and CS.

Continued

19. All equipment (cameras, etc.) is securely attached.

20. Verify communication with UAS and that the UAS has acquired GPS location (if GPS is applicable to the operation and/or aircraft).

21. Start the UAS propellers to inspect for any imbalance or irregular operation.

22. Verify all controller operations for accuracy and display of heading and altitude (if available).

23. If required by flight path walk through, verify any noted obstructions that may interfere with the UAS; and

24. At a controlled low altitude, fly within range of any interference and recheck all controls and stability.

25. Confirm any and all software, controller, or aircraft settings to ensure they have been properly set for the impending flight or mission.

1211. During the preflight inspection who is responsible for determining the aircraft is safe for flight?

A— The remote pilot in command.
B— The owner or operator.
C— The certificated mechanic who performed the annual inspection.

The remote PIC of an sUAS is responsible for determining whether that aircraft is in condition for safe flight. (PLT445) — FAA-H-8083-25

1212. How often is the remote PIC required to inspect the sUAS to ensure that it is in a condition for safe operation?

A— Annually.
B— Monthly.
C— Before each flight.

The remote PIC must inspect the sUAS before each flight. (PLT445) — 14 CFR §107.49

1213. How should an sUAS preflight inspection be accomplished for the first flight of the day?

A— Quick walk around with a check of gas and oil.
B— Thorough and systematic means recommended by the manufacturer.
C— Any sequence as determined by the pilot-in-command.

The preflight inspection should be a thorough and systematic means by which the remote PIC determines that the sUAS is ready for safe flight. Most Aircraft Flight Manuals or Pilot's Operating Handbooks contain a section on preflight inspection that should be used for guidance in this. (PLT445) — FAA-H-8083-25

1214. During your preflight inspection, you discover that the casing of your sUAS battery has expanded beyond its normal dimensions. What action should you take?

A— Throw it away with your household trash.
B— Use it as long as it will still hold a charge.
C— Follow the manufacturer's guidance.

Your first action should be to seek out the manufacturer's guidance about replacement or disposal. Do not use damaged batteries, as they may self-ignite during flight or if charged. (PLT445) — AC 107-2

1215. While preparing your sUAS for flight, you notice that one of the propeller blades has a nick. What action should you take?

A— If the nick is less than ¼ the length of the blade, it is safe to operate without replacement.
B— Remove and replace the propeller; consult manufacturer guidelines for repair, if any.
C— Repair by filing the nick to a smooth curve or with adhesive approved for use on the propeller material.

When in doubt, remove and replace any damaged part. If repair is allowed, it should be outlined by the manufacturer. Remote PICs should consult with the manufacturer about such repair. (PLT445) — AC 107-2

1216. In which of the following scenarios is a remote PIC not required to perform a preflight inspection of their sUAS?

A— If the subsequent flight occurs immediately following a flight before which an inspection was made.

B— Preflight inspections are only required for the first flight of the day, so any other flight does not require such an inspection.

C— Preflight inspections are required before each flight, thus there is no scenario that precludes such an inspection.

The remote PIC must inspect the sUAS before each flight. (PLT445) — 14 CFR §107.49

Communication Procedures

The FAA requires that the remote PIC and other crewmembers coordinate to:

1. Scan the airspace in the operational area for any potential collision hazard; and

2. Maintain awareness of the position of the sUAS through direct visual observation.

To achieve this goal, the remote PIC should:

• Foster an environment where open communication is encouraged and expected among the entire crew to maximize team performance.

• Establish effective communication procedures prior to flight.

• Select an appropriate method of communication, such as the use of hand-held radio or other effective means that would not create a distraction and allows all crewmembers to understand each other.

• Inform the crew as conditions change about any needed adjustments to ensure a safe outcome of the operation.

One way to accomplish effective communications procedures is to have a VO maintain visual contact with the small UA and maintain awareness of the surrounding airspace, and then communicate flight status and any hazards to the remote PIC and person manipulating the controls so that appropriate action can be taken. The remote PIC should evaluate which method is most appropriate for the operation and should be determined prior to flight.

Aviation has a language all its own to facilitate communication between all participants. These participants include both ATC and pilots, often communicating in a busy and noisy environment. The most important component to effective communications is understanding between the parties involved. Brevity is important, and contacts should be kept as brief as possible. Basic communication procedures include:

• Listen before you transmit.

• Think before keying your transmitter.

• Place the microphone (mic) close to your lips and after pressing the mic button, speak in a normal, conversational tone.

• Be alert both to sounds as well as a lack of sounds, which could indicate lost or broken communications.

Answers

1216 [C]

Character	Telephony	Phonic (Pronunciation)
A	Alfa	(AL-FAH)
B	Bravo	(BRAH-VOH)
C	Charlie	(CHAR-LEE) or (SHAR-LEE)
D	Delta	(DELL-TAH)
E	Echo	(ECK-OH)
F	Foxtrot	(FOKS-TROT)
G	Golf	(GOLF)
H	Hotel	(HOH-TEL)
I	India	(IN-DEE-AH)
J	Juliett	(JEW-LEE-ETT)
K	Kilo	(KEY-LOH)
L	Lima	(LEE-MAH)
M	Mike	(MIKE)
N	November	(NO-VEM-BER)
O	Oscar	(OSS-CAH)
P	Papa	(PAH-PAH)
Q	Quebec	(KEH-BECK)
R	Romeo	(ROW-ME-OH)
S	Sierra	(SEE-AIR-RAH)
T	Tango	(TANG-GO)
U	Uniform	(YOU-NEE-FORM) or (OO-NEE-FORM)
V	Victor	(VIK-TAH)
W	Whiskey	(WISS-KEY)
X	Xray	(ECKS-RAY)
Y	Yankee	(YANG-KEY)
Z	Zulu	(ZOO-LOO)
1	One	(WUN)
2	Two	(TOO)
3	Three	(TREE)
4	Four	(FOW-ER)
5	Five	(FIFE)
6	Six	(SIX)
7	Seven	(SEV-EN)
8	Eight	(AIT)
9	Nine	(NIN-ER)
0	Zero	(ZEE-RO)

Figure 5-1. Phonetic alphabet

The **phonetic alphabet** is used in aviation communications by both ATC facilities and pilots. Use the phonetic equivalents for single letters and to spell out groups of letters or difficult words during adverse communications conditions. *See* Figure 5-1.

Figures indicating hundreds and thousands in round numbers as used in weather reports or for altitudes should include both the first number of the hundred/thousand and then followed by the quantity descriptor(s). For example, "500" should be spoken "fife hundred." Another example, "4,500" should be annunciated "four thousand five hundred." The number nine is spoken "niner" and the number five is spoken "fife" to further help alleviate confusion over the radio waves and to avoid confusion among languages ("nine" sounds like the German word for no: "nein").

The three digits for course, heading or wind direction should be magnetic and spoken individually. The word "true" should be added when it applies. For example, magnetic heading 360 would be spoken "three six zero."

Speed should be followed by the words "knots" or "mile per hour." For example, the speed 87 knots is spoken "eighty-seven knots."

Time is measured in relation to the rotation of the Earth. A day is defined as the time required for the earth to make one complete revolution of 360°. Since the day is divided into 24 hours, it follows that the earth revolves at the rate of 15° each hour. Thus, lines of longitude may be expressed as 90° apart, the first of which is 6 hours west of Greenwich. Twenty-four time zones have been established. Each time zone is approximately 15° of longitude in width, with the first zone centered on the meridian of Greenwich. For most aviation operations, time is expressed in terms of the 24-hour clock (for example, 8 a.m. is expressed as 0800; 2 p.m. is 1400; 11 p.m. is 2300) and may be either local or Coordinated Universal Time (UTC). UTC is the time at the prime meridian and is represented in aviation operations by the letter "Z," referred to as "**Zulu time**" and is not adjusted for daylight savings time. For example, 1500Z would be spoken as "one five zero zero Zulu."

Initial transmissions to ATC should contain the following elements:

- Who you are—aircraft's complete call sign.
- Where you are located (either in reference to an airport, geographical location, or point on an airport).
- What you want to do or need to do—you should think about what you want to say before communicating it.

Call signs should be spoken in their entirety the first time. Never abbreviate on initial contact or any time other aircraft call signs have similar numbers/sounds or identical letters/numbers. Standard phraseology should be used at all times. *See* Figure 5-2.

When ATC authorization is required (at or near an airport with a control tower and/or when operating within controlled airspace), such permission must be requested and granted before any operation in that airspace. When ATC authorization is not required (at or near an airport without a control tower and/or when operating within uncontrolled airspace), remote PICs should monitor the CTAF to stay aware of manned aircraft communications and operations. Manned pilots will self-announce their position and intentions on the CTAF, consistent with recommended traffic advisory procedures. It is helpful to announce sUAS operations on the CTAF to increase local pilots' situational awareness, as well as potentially increase the safe interaction among manned and unmanned aircraft. Use standard phraseology at all times so as not to confuse manned pilots or other operators on the frequency.

Automatic Terminal Information Service (ATIS) is a continuous broadcast of non-control information in selected high-activity terminal areas. ATIS frequencies are listed in the *Chart Supplement U.S.* To relieve frequency congestion, pilots are urged to listen to ATIS, and on initial contact, to advise controllers that the information has been received by repeating the alphabetical code word appended to the broadcast. For example: "information Sierra received."

At airports with operating **air traffic control towers (ATCT)**, approval must be obtained prior to advancing an aircraft onto the movement area. Ground control frequencies are provided to reduce

"Acknowledge"	Let me know that you have received my message.
"Advise intentions"	Tell me what you plan to do.
"Affirmative"	Yes.
"Final"	Commonly used to mean that an aircraft is on the final approach course or is aligned with a landing area.
"Hold for"	(takeoff clearance, release, landing/taxiing aircraft, etc.) Stay in place where you are currently located.
"Hold short"	November 477ZA, runway four, taxi via Echo, hold short runway two five at taxiway Delta.
"How do you hear me?"	A question relating to the quality of the transmission or to determine how well the transmission is being received.
"Immediately"	Used by ATC or pilots when such action compliance is required to avoid an imminent situation.
"Line up and wait"	Used by ATC to inform a pilot to taxi onto the departure runway in takeoff position and LINE UP and WAIT. *It is not authorization for takeoff.* It is used when takeoff clearance cannot immediately be issued because of traffic or other reasons.
"Negative"	"No" or "permission not granted" or "that is not correct."
"Read back"	Repeat my message back to me.
"Roger"	I have received all of your last transmission. *Should not be used to answer a question requiring a yes or no answer.*
"Stand by"	Means the controller or pilot must pause for a few seconds, usually to attend to other duties of a higher priority. Also means to wait, as in "stand by for clearance." The caller should reestablish contact if a delay is lengthy. "Stand by" is not an approval or denial.
"Unable"	Indicates inability to comply with a specific instruction, request, or clearance.
"Verify"	Request confirmation of information (for example, "verify assigned altitude").
"WILCO"	I have received your message, understand it, and will comply with it.
"Without delay"	With a sense of urgency, proceed with approved instructions in a rapid manner.

Figure 5-2. Standard aviation phraseology

congestion on the tower frequency. They are used for issuance of taxi information, clearances, and other necessary contacts. If instructed by ground control to "taxi to" a particular runway, the pilot must stop prior to crossing any runway. A clearance must be obtained prior to crossing any runway. Aircraft arriving at an airport where a control tower is in operation should not change to ground control frequency until directed to do so by ATC.

The key to operating at an airport without an operating control tower is selection of the correct CTAF, which is identified in the *Chart Supplement U.S.* and on the sectional chart. CTAF is the frequency on which pilots (manned and unmanned) announce their intentions, location, or other pertinent information and monitor the intentions, location, etc. conveyed by other pilots in the area. If the airport has a part-time ATCT, the CTAF is usually a tower frequency. Where there is no tower, UNICOM, (if available) is usually the CTAF. UNICOM is limited to the necessities of safe and expeditious operation of private aircraft pertaining to runways and wind conditions, types of fuel available, weather, and dispatching. UNICOM may also transmit information concerning ground transportation, food, lodging and services available during transit. When no tower, FSS, or UNICOM is available, use the MULTICOM frequency 122.9 for self-announce procedures.

Often, there is more than one airport using the same frequency. To avoid confusion, be sure to state the airport name, followed by the term "traffic" (addressing other aircraft in the area) as part of the beginning and end of the transmission. For example, "Manatee traffic, unmanned aircraft XYZ is operating at 200 AGL approximately 3 NM south of the airport, Manatee traffic." *See* Figure 5-3.

Facility at Airport	Frequency Use	Communication/Broadcast Procedures		
		Outbound	*Inbound*	*Practice Instrument Approach*
1 UNICOM (No Tower or FSS)	Communicate with UNICOM station on published CTAF frequency (122.7, 122.8, 122.725, 122.975, or 123.0). If unable to contact UNICOM station, use self-announce procedures on CTAF.	Before taxiing and before taxiing on the runway for departure.	10 miles out. Entering downwind, base, and final. Leaving the runway.	
2 No Tower, FSS, or UNICOM	Self-announce on MULTICOM frequency 122.9.	Before taxiing and before taxiing on the runway for departure.	10 miles out. Entering downwind, base, and final. Leaving the runway.	Departing final approach fix (name) or on final approach segment inbound.
3 No Tower in operation, FSS open	Communicate with FSS on CTAF frequency.	Before taxiing and before taxiing on the runway for departure.	10 miles out. Entering downwind, base, and final. Leaving the runway.	Approach completed/terminated.
4 FSS closed (No Tower)	Self-announce on CTAF.	Before taxiing and before taxiing on the runway for departure.	10 miles out. Entering downwind, base, and final. Leaving the runway.	
5 Tower or FSS not in operation	Self-announce on CTAF.	Before taxiing and before taxiing on the runway for departure.	10 miles out. Entering downwind, base, and final. Leaving the runway.	

Figure 5-3. Summary of recommended communications procedures

Although it is unlikely that ATC will be able to track unmanned aircraft in the near future, they may issue information about traffic that is in the vicinity of sUAS operations. Traffic advisories given by ATC will refer to the other aircraft by azimuth in terms of the 12-hour clock, with 12 o'clock being the direction of flight (track), not aircraft heading. Each hourly position is equal to 30°. For example, an aircraft heading 090° is advised of traffic at the 3 o'clock position. The remote PIC (and any visual observers or crew) should look 90° to the right of the direction of flight of the sUAS, or to the south of the area of operation/UA. Remote pilots should be aware that traffic information is based upon the track observed on radar, thus if traffic advisories about your operation are conveyed to manned aircraft, they may indicate a slight difference in the perceived location of observed aircraft and the actual location of such aircraft. *See* Figure 5-4.

sUAS Frequencies

Most sUAS use radio frequencies to establish the data link between the control station and the small unmanned aircraft.

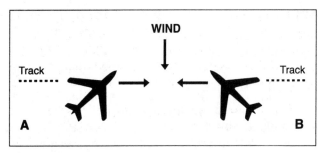

Figure 5-4. Traffic advisories are issued based on direction of flight, not the aircraft heading

Considerations for radio frequencies used in sUAS operations include:

- Frequency interference.
- Line of sight/obstructions.

The most commonly used sUAS frequencies are 2.4 GHz and 5.8 GHz. These unlicensed radio frequency bands are regulated by the Federal Communications Commission (FCC). These frequencies are also used for computer wireless networks. Therefore, frequency interference can cause problems when operating an unmanned aircraft in areas with many wireless signals (e.g., near dense housing or office buildings). Lost links and flyaways are some of the reported problems with sUAS frequency implications. To avoid frequency interference many modern sUAS operate using a 5.8 GHz system to control the sUAS, and a 2.4 GHz system to transmit video and photos to the ground. Consult the sUAS operating manual and manufacturers recommended procedures before conducting sUAS operations

Both sUAS radio frequency bands (2.4 GHz and 5.8 GHz) are considered line-of-sight. Be aware that the command and control link between the control station and the sUAS might not work properly when barriers are between the control station and the unmanned aircraft.

Radio transmissions, such as those used to control a UA and to downlink real-time video, must use frequency bands that are approved for use by the operating agency. The FCC authorizes civil operations. Some operating frequencies are unlicensed and can be used freely (e.g., 900 MHz, 2.4 GHz, and 5.8 GHz) without FCC approval. All other frequencies require a user-specific license for all civil users, except federal agencies, to be obtained from the FCC. For further information, visit **www.fcc.gov/ licensing-databases/licensing**. It is recommended that the remote PIC utilize a frequency spectrum analyzer prior to operation to ensure that there are no potential interfering transmissions in the area.

1217. Inbound to an airport with no tower, FSS, or UNICOM in operation, a pilot should self-announce on MULTICOM frequency

A— 123.0.
B— 122.9.
C— 122.7.

Where there is no tower or UNICOM station on the airport, use MULTICOM frequency 122.9 for self-announce procedures. (PLT146) — AIM ¶4-1-9

1279. The aircraft call sign N169US will be spoken in this way:

A— November one six niner uniform sierra.
B— November one six niner unmanned system.
C— November one hundred sixty nine uniform sierra.

Aircraft call signs should be spoken in their entirety, using the phonetic alphabet. Numbers are spoken individually. (PLT196) — AIM ¶4-2-3

Answers

1217 [B]   1279 [A]

1218. When flying HAWK N666CB, the proper phraseology for initial contact with Whitted ATC tower is

A— "Whitted Tower, HAWK SIX SIX SIX CHARLIE BRAVO, five NM west of the airport, request permission to enter Class D airspace for unmanned aircraft operations below four hundred AGL, three NM west of the airport"

B— "Whitted, HAWK SIX SIX SIX CEE BEE, requesting to operate within Class D, west of the field"

C— "Whitted tower, Triple Six Charlie Bravo, five NM west, operating in Class D below four hundred AGL west of the airport"

The term "initial radio contact," or "initial callup," means the first radio call you make to a given facility, or the first call to a different controller or Flight Service specialist within a facility. Use the following format:

1. *Name of facility being called;*

2. *Your full aircraft identification as filed in the flight plan;*

3. *Type of message to follow your request if it is short, and*

4. *The word "over," if required (typically omitted, except for communications via a remote communication outlet or in cases when it is necessary to confirm the end of a transmission). Example: "New York Radio, Mooney Three One One Echo, over."*

When the aircraft manufacturer's name or model is stated, the prefix "N" is dropped. The first two characters of the call sign may be dropped only after ATC calls you by your last three letters/numbers. (PLT146) — AIM ¶4-2-3

1219. The correct method of stating 4,500 feet MSL to ATC is

A— "FOUR THOUSAND FIVE HUNDRED."
B— "FOUR POINT FIVE."
C— "FORTY-FIVE HUNDRED FEET MSL."

Up to but not including 18,000 feet MSL, state the separate digits of the thousands, plus the hundreds, if appropriate. Example: "4,500—four thousand, five hundred." (PLT146) — AIM ¶4-2-9

1233. What is the best way for the remote PIC to minimize the risk of radio frequency interference during sUAS operations?

A— Never transmit on aviation frequency ranges during flight operations.
B— Monitor frequency use with a spectral analyzer.
C— Avoid the use of cellphones in the vicinity of the control station.

Remote PICs should monitor the appropriate aviation frequency such as CTAF during flight operations and make announcements concerning sUAS operations as appropriate. Some sUAS require the use of cellphone or tablet computers for operation, therefore are acceptable for use in most cases. The best way to avoid frequency interference is to check local frequency spectrum use prior to flight and continue to monitor such use during flight by utilizing a frequency spectrum analyzer. (PLT146) — AC 107-2

1220. (Refer to Figure 20, area 3.) What is the recommended communications procedure for a landing at Currituck County Airport?

A— Transmit intentions on 122.9 MHz when 10 miles out and give position reports in the traffic pattern.
B— Contact Elizabeth City FSS for airport advisory service.
C— Contact New Bern FSS for area traffic information.

Where there is no tower, Flight Service, or UNICOM station on the airport, use MULTICOM frequency 122.9 for self-announce procedures. Such airports will be identified in the appropriate aeronautical information publications. (PLT146) — AIM ¶4-1-9

1221. When should pilots state their position on the airport when calling the tower for takeoff?

A— When visibility is less than 1 mile.
B— When parallel runways are in use.
C— When departing from a runway intersection.

Pilots should state their position on the airport when calling the tower for takeoff from a runway intersection. (PLT146) — AIM ¶4-3-10

1222. As standard operating practice, all inbound and local traffic approaching or near an airport without a control tower should continuously monitor the appropriate facility from a distance of

A— 25 miles.
B— 20 miles.
C— 10 miles.

Pilots of inbound traffic should monitor and communicate as appropriate on the designated CTAF from 10 miles to landing. Pilots of departing aircraft should monitor/ communicate on the appropriate frequency from start-up, during taxi, and until 10 miles from the airport unless the regulations or local procedures require otherwise. (PLT146) — AIM ¶4-1-9

1223. Absence of the sky condition and visibility on an ATIS broadcast indicates that

A— weather conditions are at or above VFR minimums.
B— the sky condition is clear and visibility is unrestricted.
C— the ceiling is at least 5,000 feet and visibility is 5 miles or more.

The absence of a sky condition or ceiling and/or visibility on ATIS indicates a ceiling of 5,000 feet or above and visibility of 5 miles or more. (PLT196) — AIM ¶4-1-13

1224. (Refer to Figure 22 area 2; and Figure 31.) At Coeur D'Alene, which frequency should be used as a Common Traffic Advisory Frequency (CTAF) to monitor airport traffic?

A— 122.05 MHz.
B— 135.075 MHz.
C— 122.8 MHz.

CTAF is a frequency designed for the purpose of carrying out airport advisory practices and/or position reporting at an uncontrolled airport (which may also occur during hours when a tower is closed). The CTAF may be a UNICOM, MULTICOM, FSS, or tower frequency and is identified in the appropriate aeronautical publications. A solid dot with the letter "C" inside indicates CTAF. When the control tower operates part time and a UNICOM frequency is provided, use the UNICOM frequency. (PLT064) — AIM ¶4-1-9

1225. (Refer to Figure 26, area 2.) What is the recommended communication procedure when operating in the vicinity of Cooperstown Airport?

A— Broadcast intentions when 10 miles out and monitor transmissions on the CTAF/MULTICOM frequency, 122.9 MHz.
B— Contact UNICOM when 10 miles out on 122.8 MHz.
C— Circle the airport in a left turn prior to entering traffic monitoring transmissions on 122.9.

MULTICOM frequency is always 122.9 MHz, and the correct procedure is to broadcast intentions when 10 miles from the airport. (PLT146) — AIM ¶4-1-9

1308. The Common Traffic Advisory Frequency (CTAF) is used for manned aircraft to

A— announce ground and flight intentions.
B— request air traffic control clearance.
C— request fuel services.

CTAF is designed for the purpose of carrying out airport advisory practices and/or position reporting at an uncontrolled airport (which may also occur during hours when a tower is closed). The CTAF may be a UNICOM, MULTICOM, FSS, or tower frequency and is identified in the appropriate aeronautical publications. On the sectional chart, a solid dot with the letter "C" inside indicates Common Traffic Advisory Frequency. When the control tower operates part time and a UNICOM frequency is provided, use the UNICOM frequency. (PLT146) — AIM ¶4-1-9

1226. Automatic Terminal Information Service (ATIS) is the continuous broadcast of recorded information concerning

A— pilots of radar-identified aircraft whose aircraft is in dangerous proximity to terrain or to an obstruction.
B— nonessential information to reduce frequency congestion.
C— noncontrol information in selected high-activity terminal areas.

ATIS is the continuous broadcast of recorded non-control information in selected high-activity terminal areas. (PLT196) — AIM ¶4-1-13

Answers

1222 [C]   1223 [C]   1224 [C]   1225 [A]   1308 [A]   1226 [C]

1227. What services will a FSS provide?

A— Fuel pricing.
B— Assistance during an emergency.
C— Clearance to taxi for takeoff.

Flight Service Stations (FSS's) are air traffic facilities that provide pilot briefings, enroute communications and VFR search-and-rescue services, assist lost aircraft and aircraft in emergency situations, relay ATC clearances, originate Notices to Airmen, broadcast aviation weather and NAS information, receive and process IFR flight plans, and monitor NAVAIDs. In addition, FSS's take weather observations, issue airport advisories, advise Customs and Immigration of transborder flights, and provide En Route Flight Advisory Service (Flight Watch) (in Alaska only). (PLT044) — AIM ¶4-1-3

1228. You have just landed at a towered airport and the tower tells you to contact ground control when clear of the runway. You are considered clear of the runway when

A— all parts of the aircraft have crossed the hold line.
B— the aircraft cockpit is clear of the hold line.
C— the tail of the aircraft is clear of the runway edge.

An aircraft exiting a runway is not clear of the runway until all parts of the aircraft have crossed the applicable holding position marking. (PLT146) — AIM ¶2-3-5

1229. After landing at a tower controlled airport, a pilot should contact ground control

A— when advised by the tower.
B— prior to turning off the runway.
C— after reaching a taxiway that leads directly to the parking area.

A pilot who has just landed should not change from the tower frequency to the ground control frequency until directed to do so by the controller. (PLT146) — AIM ¶4-3-14

1230. An ATC radar facility issues the following advisory to a pilot flying on a heading of 090°: "UNMANNED AIRCRAFT OPERATIONS 3 O'CLOCK, 2 MILES, WESTBOUND..." Where should the Remote PIC (also visual observer and crew, if applicable) look for this traffic in reference to the UA?

A— North.
B— South.
C— West.

Traffic information will be given in azimuth from the aircraft in terms of the 12-hour clock. Thus, each hour would constitute an angle of 30°. Picture a clock in your lap; 3 o'clock is to your right, 9 o'clock is to your left, 12 o'clock is straight ahead, and 6 o'clock is behind you. If an aircraft is proceeding on a heading of 090° (east), traffic located at the 3 o'clock position would be 90° right of the nose, south of the aircraft. If the sUAS is being operated to the south of the aircraft, the aircraft itself is to the north of the operation. (PLT146) — AIM ¶4-1-15

1231. An ATC radar facility issues the following advisory to a manned aircraft pilot flying north in a calm wind: "UNMANNED AIRCRAFT OPERATIONS AT 9 O'CLOCK, 2 MILES..." Where should the Remote PIC (also visual observer and crew, if applicable) look for this traffic?

A— East.
B— North.
C— West.

An aircraft flying north in calm wind would be heading 360°. When advised of traffic at the 9 o'clock position, the pilot should look 90° left of the nose, to the west but the remote PIC and sUAS need to look to the east as they are to the west of the manned aircraft. (PLT146) — AIM ¶4-1-15

1232. A visual observer notices a manned aircraft approaching the area in which sUAS operations are taking place, flying just north of the area from west to east. What call could the remote PIC/visual observer make on CTAF to alert the manned pilot?

A— Zephyrhills traffic, unmanned aircraft Xray Yankee Zulu, operating five NM south of the airport at or below 400 AGL, located at the three o'clock position of the Cessna just north of our position, Zephyrhills traffic.
B— Zephyrhills traffic, unmanned aircraft at three o'clock of manned aircraft in the area, Zephyrhills traffic.
C— Zephyrhills traffic, unmanned aircraft Xray Yankee Zulu to Cessna in the area, look for us at your three o'clock position, we are about a mile south.

Using standard phraseology, remote PICs/crew should clearly communicate the position of the sUAS operation in relation to a known geographic location and any other information that may help the manned aircraft be aware of and avoid conflicting with the sUAS. — AIM ¶4-1-15, AC 107-2

Answers

| 1227 [B] | 1228 [A] | 1229 [A] | 1230 [A] | 1231 [A] | 1232 [A] |

Emergency Procedures

Follow any manufacturer guidance for appropriate response procedures in abnormal or emergency situations prior to flight. In case of an in-flight emergency, the remote PIC is permitted to deviate from any rule of Part 107 to the extent necessary to meet that emergency. FAA may request a written report explaining the deviation. Review emergency actions during preflight planning and inform crewmembers of their responsibilities.

The remote PIC must be prepared to respond to abnormal and emergency situations during sUAS operations. Refer to the manufacturer's guidance for appropriate procedures in the following situations:

- Abnormal situations, such as lost link, alternate landing/recovery sites, loss of GPS, loss of video link, avoidance of proximate manned or unmanned aircraft, and flight termination (controlled flight to the ground).
- Emergency situations, such as flyaways, loss of control link, avoidance of manned or unmanned aircraft in imminent danger of colliding with the sUAS, and battery fires.

Lost Link

Without an onboard pilot, sUAS crewmembers rely on the command and control link to operate the aircraft. For example, an uplink transmits command instructions to the aircraft and a downlink transmits the status of the aircraft and provides situational awareness to the remote PIC or person manipulating the controls. **Lost link** is an interruption or loss of the control link between the control station and the unmanned aircraft, preventing control of the aircraft. As a result, the unmanned aircraft may perform pre-set lost link procedures. Such procedures ensure that the unmanned aircraft:

- Remains airborne in a predictable or planned maneuver, allowing time to re-establish the communication link.
- Autolands, if available, after a predetermined length of time or terminates the flight when the power source is depleted.

A lost link is an abnormal situation, but not an emergency. A lost link is not considered a flyaway.

Follow the manufacturer's recommendations for programming lost link procedures prior to the flight. Examples of lost link procedures may include, when applicable:

- A lost link UA flies at an altitude (set by the remote PIC prior to flight) that avoids obstacles in the area or may fly a route predefined by the remote PIC.
- Communications procedures to notify crewmembers or other pertinent personnel of the loss of link.

Plan contingency measures in the event recovery of the sUAS is not feasible.

Remote PICs should conduct a thorough preflight briefing with crewmembers to discuss all lost link procedures including crewmember responsibilities and all contingency plans for abnormal and emergency situations. Contingency planning should include an alternate landing/recovery site to be used in the event of an abnormal condition that requires a precautionary landing away from the original launch location. Incorporate the means of communication with ATC throughout the descent and landing (if required for the flight operation) as well as a plan for ground operations and securing/parking the aircraft on the ground. This includes the availability of control stations capable of launch/recovery, communication equipment, and an adequate power source to operate all required equipment. Take into consideration all airspace constructs and minimize risk to other aircraft by avoiding persons, congested areas, and other aircraft to the maximum extent possible.

Continued

Flight Termination

Flight termination is the intentional and deliberate process of performing controlled flight to the ground. Flight termination may be part of lost link procedures, or it may be a contingency that you elect to use if further flight of the aircraft cannot be safely achieved, or if other potential hazards exist that require immediate discontinuation of flight. Execute flight termination procedures if you have exhausted all other contingencies. **Flight termination points (FTPs)**, if used, or alternative contingency planning measures must:

- Be located within power-off glide distance (fixed wing) or low-power rapid descent (rotor wing) of the aircraft during all phases of flight;
- Be based on the assumption of an unrecoverable system failure;
- Take into consideration altitude, winds, and other factors; and
- Take into consideration obstacles, persons, congested areas, and other aircraft operations.

Flyaways

A **flyaway** often begins as a lost link—an interruption or loss of the control link prevents control of the aircraft. As a result, the unmanned aircraft is not operating in a predicable or planned manner. However, in a flyaway, the pre-set lost link procedures are not established or are not being executed by the unmanned aircraft, creating an emergency situation. In rare instances, software or hardware malfunctions may induce a flyaway. If a flyaway occurs while operating in airspace that requires authorization, notify ATC as outlined in the authorization.

Loss of GPS

GPS tools can be a valuable resource for flight planning and situational awareness during sUAS operation. However, as with manned aviation, remote PICs in sUAS operations must avoid overreliance on automation and must be prepared to operate the unmanned aircraft manually, if necessary.

- Prior to flight, check NOTAMs for any known GPS service disruptions in the planned location of the sUAS operation. Most sUAS have the ability to operate without significant degradation of control if GPS signals are not available or are lost in flight (contingency planning should include such scenarios).
- Make a plan of action to prevent or minimize damage in the event of equipment malfunction or failure.

Battery Fires

Battery fires pose a significant hazard to sUAS. Because sUAS often utilize high energy density, rechargeable batteries, the risk for battery malfunction or failure are real concerns for sUAS operations. The charge/discharge cycle involves significant changes in temperature which can stress internal components of the battery. Before each flight, batteries should be inspected for any obvious damage, bloating or deformation, and excessive heat.

Both lithium metal and lithium-ion batteries are:

- Highly flammable;
- Capable of self-ignition when a battery short circuits or is overcharged, heated to extreme temperatures, mishandled, or otherwise defective; and
- Subject to thermal runaway.

Thermal runaway usually occurs during a rapid discharge event such as a short or structural failure within in battery cell. During thermal runaway, lithium batteries generate sufficient heat to cause adjacent cells to also go into thermal runaway. Once in thermal runaway, the battery may hiss (release gas), smoke, catch fire, or explode. Fires with these types of batteries are very difficult to extinguish. Because lithium can react with water, it is inadvisable to use water to aid in extinguishing the fire. Type D fire extinguishers, designed for chemical and combustible metal fires are recommended to assist in fire suppression. Covering the battery in sand can also help smother the fire. Batteries should be charged and stored in battery bags specifically designed to contain battery failures. As with any component, follow manufacturer guidelines and cautions prior to and during use.

Ensure careful storage of spare (uninstalled) lithium batteries. Take the following precautions to prevent a battery fire:

- Prevent short circuits by placing each individual battery in the original retail packaging, a separate plastic bag, a protective pouch, or by insulating exposed terminals with tape.
- Do not allow spare batteries to come in contact with metal objects, such as coins, keys, or jewelry.
- Take steps to prevent objects from crushing, puncturing, or applying pressure on the battery.

When preparing to conduct sUAS operations, do not charge or use any battery with signs of damage or defect. For example, check carefully for small nicks in the battery casing and be alert for signs of bubbling or warping during charging. Once the battery is installed and the sUAS takes flight, the remote PIC or ground crew might not observe a battery fire until it is too late to land the aircraft safely. If a battery fire occurs, follow any manufacturer guidance for response procedures. Following flight, allow the battery to cool prior to charging or storing (allow it to return to room temperature).

When disposing of a used or damaged battery, follow the manufacturer and local trash collection guidelines, as these types of devices are typically considered hazardous materials and should not be treated as regular trash for disposal.

1234. Damaged lithium batteries can cause

A— an inflight fire.
B— a change in aircraft center of gravity
C— increased endurance.

Both lithium metal and lithium-ion batteries are highly flammable and capable of self-ignition when a battery short circuits or is overcharged, heated to extreme temperatures, mishandled, or otherwise defective. (PLT208) — SAFO 10017

1235. Which of the following lithium batteries should not be used?

A— A partially discharged battery that is warm from recent prior use.
B— A new battery that has only been charged once, several charging cycles are required prior to normal use.
C— A battery with a bulge on one of the sides of its case.

Damaged batteries should never be used or charged. Lithium batteries do normally get warm during discharge. Avoid the use of hot batteries. New batteries should be treated per manufacturing instructions, but do not normally need several charge cycles to use. (PLT208) — SAFO 10017

1236. What is the proper response by the remote PIC if experiencing a lost link situation?

A— Notify all available crew and ATC (if applicable) while executing the briefed lost link procedure.
B— Wait for the unit to reestablish link while notifying local law enforcement of possible dangers to nonparticipants.
C— Turning the control station off and then back on to attempt the reestablishment of the link.

All participants in the sUAS operation and ATC (if operating within or near controlled airspace) should be notified of the lost link situation. In most cases this is not considered an emergency however, if at anytime it appears that lost link may result in a flyaway or other type of dangerous situation, an emergency should be declared. There is no obligation to contact local law enforcement. It is never recommended to turn off the control station when the UA engines are running or if it is in flight. (PLT208) — AC 107-2, 14 CFR §107.21

Answers

1234 [A]   1235 [C]   1236 [A]

1237. Which of the following events is considered a flyaway?

A— Loss of link between the remote PIC and the unmanned aircraft.

B— Loss of communication link between the Remote PIC and ATC.

C— Unmanned aircraft does not respond to control inputs and does not execute known lost link maneuvers.

A flyaway is when the sUAS becomes uncontrollable and does not operate in a manner that would be expected in a normal or lost link flight situation. (PLT208) — 14 CFR Part 107

1238. What action should be taken by the remote PIC during a sUAS flyaway event?

A— Immediately notify the NTSB.

B— Immediately notify any/all crewmembers, bystanders, and ATC (if applicable).

C— Immediately notify any/all crewmembers, local law enforcement personnel, and bystanders.

During a flyaway event, sUAS may not react in ways that can be expected or predicted, thus this is an emergency situation. The remote PIC should immediately communicate this emergency to crewmembers and ATC (if applicable) as well as any persons in the immediate area so as to minimize risk for injury. There is no obligation to contact the NTSB or law enforcement during a flyaway, (PL208) — 14 CFR §§107.19 and 107.21

1239. A common cause of sUAS flyaway events is

A— frequency interference.

B— loss of GPS signals.

C— persons standing close to the control station antenna.

Frequency interference is one of the most common causes of flyaways; therefore remote PICs should assess the risk of such interference prior to and during flight. Extra caution is necessary when operating in the vicinity of other sUAS. The loss of GPS may degrade the sUAS capabilities slightly but should not cause a flyaway. It is not unusual for people to stand near the control station; it is highly unlikely for this to cause a flyaway. (PLT208) — AC 107-2

1240. Upon GPS signal loss, the remote pilot should immediately

A— contact ATC and declare an emergency.

B— perform the planned lost link contingency procedure.

C— operate the sUAS normally, noting to account for any mode or control changes that occur if GPS is lost.

Most sUAS are designed to fly normally with minimal impact on features or controllability if GPS signals are degraded or lost. Loss of GPS is not an emergency and is not considered to be a loss of link between the unmanned aircraft and the control station. If the failure of GPS does result in a flyaway or other dangerous situation, it should be treated as an emergency. (PLT208) — AC 107-2

1241. What action should the remote PIC take upon GPS signal loss?

A— Perform the planned flyaway emergency procedure.

B— Follow normal sUAS operational procedures, noting any mode or control changes that normally occur if GPS is lost.

C— Land the unmanned aircraft immediately prior to loss of control.

Most sUAS are designed to fly normally with minimal impact on features or controllability if GPS signals are degraded or lost. Loss of GPS is not an emergency and is not considered to be a flyaway situation nor does it require the sUAS operation to be terminated (unless specified by the manufacturer). If the failure of GPS does result in a flyaway or other dangerous situation, it should be treated as an emergency. (PLT208) — AC 107-2

Answers

1237 [C]	1238 [B]	1239 [A]	1240 [C]	1241 [B]

Aeronautical Decision Making

A remote PIC should use a variety of different resources to safely operate an sUAS and needs to be able to manage these resources effectively. An sUAS operation may involve one individual or a team of crewmembers, as follows:

- The remote PIC who holds a current Remote Pilot certificate with an sUAS rating and has the final authority and responsibility for the operation and safety of the sUAS;
- A person manipulating the controls operates the sUAS under direct supervision of the remote PIC;
- A VO acts as a flight crewmember to help see and avoid air traffic or other objects in the sky, overhead, or on the ground; and/or
- Other persons associated with the operation of the sUAS acting as part of the designated crew.

A culture of safety must be established with all commercial sUAS operations. Many techniques from manned aircraft operations apply to the operation of unmanned aircraft. Examples include situational awareness, risk-based **aeronautical decision making (ADM)**, **crew resource management (CRM)**, and safety management systems.

The remote PIC attains situational awareness by obtaining as much information as possible prior to a flight and becoming familiar with the performance capabilities of the sUAS, weather conditions, surrounding airspace, privacy issues, and ATC requirements. Sources of information include a weather briefing, ATC, FAA, local pilots, local laws and ordinances, as well as landowners.

Technology, such as GPS, mapping systems, and computer applications, can assist in collecting and managing information to improve your situational awareness and risk-based ADM. ADM is a systematic approach to the mental process used by pilots to consistently determine the best course of action in response to a given set of circumstances.

Crew resource management is the effective use of all available resources—human, hardware, and information—prior to and during flight to ensure a successful outcome of the operation. The remote PIC must integrate CRM techniques into all phases of the sUAS operation. Many of these techniques traditionally used in manned aircraft operations are also applicable for sUAS, such as the ability to:

- Delegate operational tasks and manage crewmembers;
- Recognize and address hazardous attitudes;
- Establish effective team communication procedures; and
- Be open to questions and concerns of any and all crewmembers.

Risk management is part of the decision-making process which relies on situational awareness, problem recognition, and good judgment to reduce risks associated with each flight. Sound risk management skills will help prevent and break the final "link" in the accident chain.

A **safety management system (SMS)** is the formal, top-down business-like approach to managing safety risk, which includes a systemic approach to managing safety, including the necessary organizational structures, accountabilities, policies and procedures.

The remote PIC identifies, delegates, and manages tasks for each sUAS operation. Tasks can vary greatly depending on the complexity of the sUAS operation. Supporting crewmembers can help accomplish those tasks and ensure the safety of flight. For example, visual observers and other ground crew can provide valuable information about traffic, airspace, weather, equipment, and aircraft loading and performance. The remote PIC:

Continued

- Assesses the operating environment (airspace, surrounding terrain, weather, hazards, etc.).
- Determines the appropriate number of crewmembers that are needed to safely conduct a given operation. The remote PIC must ensure sufficient crew support so that no one on the team becomes over-tasked, which increases the possibility of an incident or accident.
- Informs participants of delegated tasks and sets expectations.
- Manages and supervises the crew to ensure that everyone completes their assigned tasks.

Hazardous attitudes can affect unmanned operations if the remote PIC is not aware of the hazards, leading to situations such as:

- Falling behind in the progress of the aircraft/situation;
- Operating without adequate fuel/battery reserve;
- Loss of positional or situational awareness;
- Operating outside the unmanned aircraft flight envelope; and
- Failure to complete all flight planning tasks, preflight inspections, and checklists.

Operational pressure is a contributor to becoming subject to these pitfalls. Studies have identified five hazardous attitudes that can interfere with the ability to make sound decisions and properly exercise authority: anti-authority, impulsivity, invulnerability, "machoism," and resignation. *See* Figure 5-5. Remote PICs should be alert to recognize hazardous attitudes (in themselves or in other crewmembers), bring attention to and label actions deemed to be hazardous, and correct the behavior.

Attitude	Motto	Indicators
Anti-authority	"Don't tell me what to do."	The person does not like or may resent anyone telling him or her what to do. The person may regard rules, regulations, and procedures as silly or unnecessary. (Note: it is always your prerogative to question authority if you feel it is in error.)
Impulsivity	"Do it quickly."	The person frequently feels the need to do something, anything, immediately. He or she does not stop to think about the best alternative and does the first thing that comes to mind.
Invulnerability	"It won't happen to me."	The person falsely believes that accidents happen to others, but never to him or her. The person knows accidents can happen and that anyone can be affected. However, the person never really feels or believes that he or she will be personally involved. Such people are more likely than others to take chances and increase risk.
Machoism	"I can do it—I'll show them."	The person tries to prove that he or she is better than anyone else. The person takes risks to impress others. (Note: While this pattern is thought to be a male characteristic, females are equally susceptible.)
Resignation	"What's the use?"	The person does not believe his or her actions make a difference in what happens. The person attributes outcomes to good or bad luck. He or she leaves the action to others, for better or worse. Sometimes, the person even goes along with unreasonable requests just to be a "nice guy."

Figure 5-5. Hazardous attitudes

Identifying associated hazards is the first step to mitigating the hazardous attitude. Analyzing the likelihood and severity of the hazards occurring establishes the probability of risk. In most cases, risk management steps can be taken to mitigate, even eliminate, those risks. Actions such as using visual observers, completing a thorough preflight inspection, planning for weather, familiarity with the airspace, proper aircraft loading, and performance planning can mitigate identified risks. Take advantage of information from a weather briefing, ATC, the FAA, local pilots, and landowners. Technology can aid in decision-making and improve situational awareness. Being able to collect the information from these resources and manage the information is key to situational awareness and could have a positive effect on your decision-making.

It is also beneficial for remote PICs to assess risk for each mission or type of operation. Guidance on how to conduct such an evaluation is available from the US Geological Survey and can be found at **www.asa2fly.com/reader/TPUAS**. This can focus attention on actions or parts of the mission that may entail the highest risk and therefore can be actively mitigated with proper planning, ADM, and CRM.

1242. The effective use of all available resources—human, hardware, and information—prior to and during flight to ensure the successful outcome of the operation is called

A—risk management.
B—crew resource management.
C—safety management system.

Crew resource management is the effective use of all available resources—human, hardware, and information—prior to and during flight to ensure a successful outcome of the operation. (PLT104) — AC 107-2

Answer (A) is incorrect because risk management is part of the decision-making process which relies on situational awareness, problem recognition, and good judgment to reduce risks associated with each flight. Answer (C) is incorrect because Safety Management System (SMS) is the formal, top-down business-like approach to managing safety risk, which includes a systemic approach to managing safety, including the necessary organizational structures, accountabilities, policies and procedures.

1243. When adapting crew resource management (CRM) concepts to the operation of a small unmanned aircraft, CRM must be integrated into

A—the communications only.
B—the flight portion only.
C—all phases of the operation.

Crew resource management is the effective use of all available resources—human, hardware, and information—prior to and during flight to ensure a successful outcome of the operation. The remote PIC must integrate crew resource management techniques into all phases of the sUAS operation. (PLT104) — FAA-H-8083-25

1244. Safety is an important element for a remote pilot to consider prior to operating an unmanned aircraft system. To prevent the final "link" in the accident chain, a remote pilot must consider which methodology?

A—Crew resource management.
B—Safety management system.
C—Risk management.

Risk management is the part of the decision making process that relies on situational awareness, problem recognition, and good judgment to reduce the risks associated with each flight. (PLT104) — FAA-H-8083-25

Answers (A) and (B) are incorrect because CRM and SMS will incorporate risk management as part of their process.

1245. A local TV station has hired a remote pilot to operate their small UA to cover breaking news stories. The remote pilot has had multiple near misses with obstacles on the ground and two small UAS accidents. What would be a solution for the news station to improve their operating safety culture?

A—The news station should implement a policy of no more than five crashes/incidents within 6 months.
B—The news station does not need to make any changes; there are times that an accident is unavoidable.
C—The news station should recognize hazardous attitudes and situations and develop standard operating procedures that emphasize safety.

A culture of safety must be established with all commercial sUAS operations. This safety culture may use a number of techniques including situational awareness, risk-based aeronautical decision making (ADM), crew resource management (CRM), and safety management systems (SMS). (PLT271) — FAA-H-8083-25

Answers

1242 [B]   1243 [C]   1244 [C]   1245 [C]

1246. Identify the hazardous attitude or characteristic a remote pilot in command displays while taking risks in order to impress others?

A— Impulsivity.
B— Invulnerability.
C— Machoism.

Machoism, as a hazardous attitude, has the motto "I can do it, I'll show them." The person tries to prove that he or she is better than anyone else. The person takes risks to impress others. (PLT103) — FAA-H-8083-25

1247. You have been hired as a remote pilot in command by a local TV news station to film breaking news with a small unmanned aircraft. You expressed a safety concern and the station manager has instructed you to "fly first, ask questions later." What type of hazardous attitude does this attitude represent?

A— Invulnerability.
B— Impulsivity.
C— Machoism.

Impulsivity, as a hazardous attitude, has the motto "Do it quickly." The person frequently feels the need to do something, anything, immediately. He or she does not stop to think about the best alternative and does the first thing that comes to mind. (PLT103) — FAA-H-8083-25

1248. What antidotal phrase can help reverse the hazardous attitude of "antiauthority"?

A— Rules do not apply in this situation.
B— I know what I am doing.
C— Follow the rules.

The antiauthority (don't tell me!) attitude is found in people who do not like anyone telling them what to do. The antidote for this attitude is: follow the rules, they are usually right. (PLT103) — FAA-H-8083-25

1249. Hazardous attitudes occur to every pilot to some degree at some time. What are some of these hazardous attitudes?

A— Poor risk management and lack of stress management.
B— Antiauthority, impulsivity, macho, resignation, and invulnerability.
C— Poor situational awareness, snap judgments, and lack of a decision making process.

ADM addresses the following five hazardous attitudes: antiauthority (don't tell me!), impulsivity (do something quickly!), invulnerability (it won't happen to me!), machoism (I can do it!), and resignation (what's the use?). (PLT103) — FAA-H-8083-25

1250. Risk management, as part of the aeronautical decision making (ADM) process, relies on which features to reduce the risks associated with each flight?

A— Application of stress management and risk element procedures.
B— Situational awareness, problem recognition, and good judgment.
C— The mental process of analyzing all information in a particular situation and making a timely decision on what action to take.

Risk management is the part of the decision-making process which relies on situational awareness, problem recognition, and good judgment to reduce risks associated with each flight. (PLT104) — FAA-H-8083-25

1251. To avoid missing important steps, always use the

A— appropriate checklists.
B— placarded airspeeds.
C— airworthiness certificate.

To avoid missing important steps, always use the appropriate checklists whenever they are available. Consistent adherence to approved checklists is a sign of a disciplined and competent pilot. (PLT104) — FAA-H-8083-25

1252. An extreme case of a pilot getting behind the aircraft can lead to the operational pitfall of

A— loss of situational awareness.
B— loss of workload.
C— internal stress.

"Getting behind the aircraft," or falling behind in the progress of a flight, can result in not knowing where you are, an inability to recognize deteriorating circumstances, and/or the misjudgment of the rate of deterioration. (PLT104) — FAA-H-8083-25

Answers

1246 [C]   1247 [B]   1248 [C]   1249 [B]   1250 [B]   1251 [A]
1252 [A]

1253. Which statement is not correct concerning crew resource management in sUAS operations?

A— Crewmembers cannot, under any circumstances, challenge the decisions of the Remote PIC.

B— Individuals who are exhibiting signs of hazardous attitudes should be approached about the issue.

C— The remote PIC and all crewmembers should communicate any observed hazards or concerns to one another.

Crewmembers should express any and all concerns about decisions of the remote PIC or other crewmembers at any time. Clearly, the remote PIC is in charge, but that does not always make them right or invulnerable to errors, omissions, or other potentially hazardous instances. (PLT104) — FAA-H-8083-25

Answers (B) and (C) are incorrect because these are of favorable CRM interactions.

1291. What antidotal phrase can help reverse the hazardous attitude of impulsivity?

A— It could happen to me.

B— Do it quickly to get it over with.

C— Not so fast, think first.

Impulsivity (do something quickly!) is the attitude of people who frequently feel the need to do something, anything, immediately. They do not stop to think about what they are about to do, they do not select the best alternative, and they do the first thing that comes to mind. The antidote for this attitude is: Not so fast. Think first. (PLT103) — FAA-H-8083-25

1299. What is the best way to mitigate risk?

A— SMS plan.

B— Weekly meetings.

C— Establishing an operational procedure guideline.

To fly safely, the pilot needs to assess the degree of risk and determine the best course of action to mitigate the risk. (PLT104) — FAA-H-8083-25

1315. The accurate perception and understanding of all the risk element factors and conditions is

A— situational awareness.

B— judgment.

C— aeronautical decision making.

Situational awareness is the accurate perception and understanding of all the factors and conditions within the five fundamental risk elements (flight, pilot, aircraft, environment, and type of operation that comprise any given aviation situation) that affect safety before, during, and after the flight. (PLT104) — FAA-H-8083-25

Physiology

Remote pilots are not required to hold a medical certificate. However, no person may manipulate the flight controls of an sUAS or act as a remote PIC, visual observer, or direct participant in the operation of the small unmanned aircraft if he or she knows or has reason to know that he or she has a physical or mental condition that would interfere with the safe operation of the sUAS. Remote pilots must self-assess their fitness for flight. Pilot performance can be seriously degraded by a number of physiological factors. While some of the factors may be beyond the control of the pilot, awareness of cause and effect can help minimize any adverse effects. At any time a remote PIC determines that him/herself or another crewmember is unfit to operate the sUAS or participate in its operation, the remote PIC should terminate the operation and/or follow contingency plans for such occasions (e.g., incapacitation).

Hyperventilation, a deficiency of carbon dioxide within the body, can be the result of rapid or extra deep breathing due to emotional tension, anxiety, or fear. Symptoms will subside after the rate and depth of breathing are brought under control. A pilot should be able to overcome the symptoms or avoid future occurrences of hyperventilation by talking aloud, breathing into a bag, or slowing the breathing rate.

Continued

Answers

1253 [A]	1291 [C]	1299 [C]	1315 [A]

The sUAS operating environment can be very extreme for crewmembers. It is not uncommon for sUAS operations to take place in hot, dry and dusty locations, which can lead to dehydration and/or heat stroke. Alternatively, sUAS also operate in cold or other conditions that leave crewmembers exposed to the elements that could lead to dehydration and hypothermia. **Dehydration** is the term given to a critical loss of water from the body. Causes of dehydration are environmental conditions, wind, humidity, and diuretic drinks (i.e., coffee, tea, alcohol, and caffeinated soft drinks). Some common signs of dehydration are headache, fatigue, cramps, sleepiness, and dizziness. To help prevent dehydration, drink two to four quarts of water every 24 hours.

Heatstroke is a condition caused by any inability of the body to control its temperature. Onset of this condition may be recognized by the symptoms of dehydration, but also has been known to be recognized only upon complete collapse.

Hypothermia is indicated by shivering, clumsiness, slurred speech, confusion, low energy, discoloration of the skin (red or blue), and loss of consciousness. Remote PICs should ensure that they and their fellow crewmembers are adequately prepared for the planned sUAS operation and the environment in which this operation is set to take place. Some things to keep in mind are: providing ample water or other hydrating beverages, eye protection, sun protection, insect repellent, warm clothes or clothes suited for heat (whichever is appropriate), support equipment, and any other items deemed necessary for safety and comfort.

Stress is ever present in our lives and you may already be familiar with situations that create stress in aviation. However, sUAS operations may create stressors that differ from manned aviation. Such examples may include: working with an inexperienced crewmember, lack of standard crewmember training, interacting with the public and government officials, and understanding new regulatory requirements. Proper planning for the operation can reduce or eliminate stress, allowing you to focus more clearly on the operation.

Fatigue is frequently associated with pilot error. Some of the effects of fatigue include degradation of attention and concentration, impaired coordination, and decreased ability to communicate. These factors seriously influence the ability to make effective decisions. Physical fatigue results from sleep loss, exercise, or physical work. Factors such as stress and prolonged performance of cognitive work can result in mental fatigue. Fatigue falls into two broad categories: acute and chronic. **Acute fatigue** is short term and is a normal occurrence in everyday living. It is the kind of tiredness people feel after a period of strenuous effort, excitement, or lack of sleep. Rest after exertion and 8 hours of sound sleep ordinarily cures this condition. **Chronic fatigue** is characterized by extreme fatigue or tiredness that doesn't go away with rest, and can't be explained by an underlying medical condition. Chronic fatigue can also occur when there is not enough time for a full recovery from repeated episodes of acute fatigue.

Chronic stress results with longer-term stresses and/or the mismanagement thereof and can result in serious health conditions such as anxiety, high blood pressure, a weakened immune system, depression, confusion, mental errors, insomnia, and memory loss. The best way to cope with chronic stress is to remove stressors as much as practical, take part in physical activity, and/or seek out the advice or care of a healthcare provider.

Vision is the most important body sense for safe flight. Major factors that determine how effectively vision can be used are the level of illumination and the technique of scanning the sky for other aircraft. Atmospheric haze and fog reduces the ability to see traffic or terrain during flight, making all features appear to be farther away than they actually are. Caution is always advised in areas of reduced visibility or low light.

Additionally, the remote PIC and crewmembers should take into account the impact the environment may have on vision, such as location and angle of the sun, the color and texture of the local terrain features, as well as glare from water, buildings, or other objects. Particular caution is advised when operating near terrain features which may make it difficult to distinguish the sUAS from the surrounding environment or may make it difficult to ascertain proper depth perception (for example, terrain colors similar to the unmanned aircraft or a large area of trees which may make it more challenging to determine the distance between the unmanned aircraft and the foliage).

1254. Who is responsible for determining whether a pilot is fit to fly for a particular flight, even though he or she holds a current medical certificate?

A— The FAA.
B— The medical examiner.
C— The pilot.

The pilot is responsible for determining whether he or she is fit to fly for a particular flight. (PLT098) — FAA-H-8083-25

1255. You are a remote pilot in command for a co-op energy service provider. You plan to use your unmanned aircraft to inspect powerlines in the remote area 15 hours away from your home office. After the drive, fatigue impacts your abilities to complete your assignment on time. What kind of fatigue is this?

A— Chronic fatigue.
B— Acute fatigue.
C— Exhaustion.

Acute fatigue is short term and is a normal occurrence in everyday living. It is the kind of tiredness people feel after a period of strenuous effort, excitement, or lack of sleep. (PLT272) — FAA-H-8083-25

1302. What can affect your performance?

A— Prescription medications.
B— Over-the-counter medications.
C— Over-the-counter and prescribed medications.

Virtually all medications have the potential for adverse side effects in some people. (PLT205) — FAA-H-8083-25

1256. Fatigue can be recognized

A— easily by an experienced pilot.
B— as being in an impaired state.
C— by an ability to overcome sleep deprivation.

The fatigued pilot is an impaired pilot, and flying requires unimpaired judgment. (PLT272) — FAA-H-8083-2

1257. Fatigue can be either

A— physiological or psychological.
B— physical or mental.
C— acute or chronic.

Fatigue can be either acute (short-term) or chronic (long-term). Acute fatigue, a normal occurrence of everyday living, is the tiredness felt after long periods of physical and mental strain, including strenuous muscular effort, immobility, heavy mental workload, strong emotional pressure, monotony, and lack of sleep. Chronic fatigue occurs when there is not enough time for a full recovery from repeated episodes of acute fatigue. (PLT272) — FAA-H-8083-25

1258. Fatigue is one of the most treacherous hazards to flight safety

A— because it results in slow performance.
B— as it may not be apparent until serious errors are made.
C— as it may be a function of physical robustness or mental acuity.

Fatigue is one of the most treacherous hazards to flight safety as it may not be apparent to a pilot until serious errors are made. (PLT272) — FAA-H-8083-25

1259. When a stressful situation is encountered in flight, an abnormal increase in the volume of air breathed in and out can cause a condition known as

A— hyperventilation.
B— aerosinusitis.
C— aerotitis.

An abnormal increase in the volume of air breathed in and out of the lungs flushes an excessive amount of carbon dioxide from the lungs and blood, causing hyperventilation. (PLT332) — AIM ¶8-1-3

1260. Which would most likely result in hyperventilation?

A— Emotional tension, anxiety, or fear.

B— The excessive consumption of alcohol.

C— An extremely slow rate of breathing and insufficient oxygen.

Hyperventilation is most likely to occur during periods of stress or anxiety. (PLT332) — AIM ¶8-1-3

1261. Which will almost always affect your ability to fly?

A— Over-the-counter analgesics and antihistamines.

B— Antibiotics and anesthetic drugs.

C— Prescription analgesics and antihistamines.

Pilot performance can be seriously degraded by both prescribed and over-the-counter medications, as well as by the medical conditions for which they are taken. Flying is almost always precluded while using prescription analgesics since these drugs may cause side effects such as mental confusion, dizziness, headaches, nausea, and vision problems. Depressants, including antihistamines, lower blood pressure, reduce mental processing, and slow motor and reaction responses. (PLT463) — FAA-H-8083-25

Answer (A) is incorrect because over-the-counter analgesics such as aspirin, Tylenol® and Advil®, and non-drowsy antihistamines (Claritin®, Allegra®, etc.) have few side effects when taken in the correct dosage. Answer (B) is incorrect because these drugs do not typically limit flying (but the medical conditions for which they are being taken may indeed limit flying activities).

1262. As a pilot, flying for long periods in hot summer temperatures increases the susceptibility of dehydration since the

A— dry air at altitude tends to increase the rate of water loss from the body.

B— moist air at altitude helps retain the body's moisture.

C— temperature decreases with altitude.

As a pilot, flying for long periods in hot summer temperatures or at high altitudes increases the susceptibility of dehydration since the dry air at altitude tends to increase the rate of water loss from the body. If this fluid is not replaced, fatigue progresses to dizziness, weakness, nausea, tingling of hands and feet, abdominal cramps, and extreme thirst. (PLT098) — FAA-H-8083-25

1273. Which would most likely result in hyperventilation?

A— Insufficient oxygen.

B— Excessive carbon monoxide.

C— Insufficient carbon dioxide.

As hyperventilation 'blows off' excessive carbon dioxide from the body, a pilot can experience symptoms of lightheadedness, suffocation, drowsiness, tingling of the extremities, and coolness and react to them with even greater hyperventilation. (PLT332) — FAA-H-8083-25

Answer (A) is incorrect because insufficient oxygen is a symptom of hypoxia. Answer (B) is incorrect because excessive carbon monoxide will lead to carbon monoxide poisoning.

1263. When setting up the location of the control station and placement of crewmembers for an afternoon flight, which of the following would be most appropriate for ensuring that vision is not impaired by the environment?

A— The operation should be set up so that the remote PIC and crewmembers can face east.

B— The operation should be set up so that the remote PIC and crewmembers can face west.

C— The operation should be set up so that the remote PIC and crewmembers are facing any reflective objects in the area.

If the operation is to take place in the afternoon, the sun will be setting towards the west and could impair the vision of those participating in the sUAS operation. Thus, when practical, the operation should be set up to minimize the impact of the sun on being able to maintain visual line-of-sight with the unmanned aircraft. (PLT333) — FAA-H-8083-25, 14 CFR §107.31

Answer (B) is incorrect because persons will have the sun in their eyes. Answer (C) is incorrect because it potentially will present glare or reflections into the eyes of participants.

1297. What can help a pilot mitigate stress?

A— Increasing stress tolerance.

B— Removing stress from personal life.

C— Breathing into a paper bag.

There are several techniques to help manage the accumulation of life stresses and prevent stress overload. For example, to help reduce stress levels, set aside time for relaxation each day or maintain a program of physical fitness. To prevent stress overload, learn to manage time more effectively to avoid pressures imposed by getting behind schedule and not meeting deadlines. (PLT272) — FAA-H-8083-25

Answers

1260 [A]	1261 [C]	1262 [A]	1273 [C]	1263 [A]	1297 [B]

1264. When setting up the location of the control station and placement of crewmembers for a flight over snowy terrain, which of the following would be most appropriate for ensuring that vision is not impaired by the environment?

A— The operation should be set up so that the crewmembers are the most comfortable.

B— The operation should be set up so that the crewmembers will experience the minimum glare from the snow.

C— The operation should be set up so that the crewmembers face the direction in which the terrain most closely matches the color of the unmanned aircraft.

If the operation is to take place in a snow covered environment, awareness concerning how this may impact vision, such as glare or the ability to see and operate the unmanned aircraft against a featureless background. Thus, when practical, the operation should be set up to minimize the impact of the terrain on being able to maintain visual line-of-sight with the unmanned aircraft. (PLT333) — FAA-H-8083-25, 14 CFR §107.31

Answer (A) is incorrect because while comfort is important, maintaining visual line-of-sight and positive control over the unmanned aircraft is more critical. Answer (C) is incorrect because it may make it difficult to keep the unmanned aircraft in sight, distinguished from the background, and/or may result in loss of depth perception.

Maintenance and Inspection Procedures

Maintenance for sUAS includes scheduled and unscheduled overhaul, repair, inspection, modification, replacement, and system software upgrades for the unmanned aircraft itself and all components necessary for flight.

Manufacturers may recommend a maintenance or replacement schedule for the unmanned aircraft and system components based on time-in-service limits and other factors. Follow all manufacturer maintenance recommendations to achieve the longest and safest service life of the sUAS. If the sUAS or component manufacturer does not provide scheduled maintenance instructions, it is recommended that you establish your own scheduled maintenance protocol. For example:

* Document any repair, modification, overhaul, or replacement of a system component resulting from normal flight operations.

* Record the time-in-service for that component at the time of the maintenance procedure.

* Assess these records over time to establish a reliable maintenance schedule for the sUAS and its components.

During the course of a preflight inspection, you may discover that an sUAS component requires some form of maintenance outside of the scheduled maintenance period. For example, an sUAS component may require servicing (such as lubrication), repair, modification, overhaul, or replacement as a result of normal or abnormal flight operations. Or, the sUAS manufacturer or component manufacturer may require an unscheduled system software update to correct a problem. In the event such a condition is found, do not conduct flight operations until the discrepancy is corrected.

In some instances, the sUAS or component manufacturer may require certain maintenance tasks be performed by the manufacturer or by a person or facility specified by the manufacturer; maintenance should be performed in accordance with the manufacturer's instructions. However, if you decide not to use the manufacturer or the personnel recommended by the manufacturer and you are unable to perform the required maintenance yourself, you should:

* Solicit the expertise of maintenance personnel familiar with the specific sUAS and its components.

* Consider using certificated maintenance providers, such as repair stations, holders of mechanic and repairman certificates, and persons working under the supervision of a mechanic or repairman.

Continued

Answers

1264 **[B]**

If you or the maintenance personnel are unable to repair, modify, or overhaul an sUAS or component back to its safe operational specification, then it is advisable to replace the sUAS or component with one that is in a condition for safe operation. Complete all required maintenance before each flight—preferably in accordance with the manufacturer's instructions or, in lieu of that, within known industry best practices.

Careful recordkeeping can be highly beneficial for sUAS owners and operators. For example, recordkeeping provides essential safety support for commercial operators who may experience rapidly accumulated flight operational hours/cycles. Consider maintaining a hardcopy and/or electronic logbook of all periodic inspections, maintenance, preventative maintenance, repairs, and alterations performed on the sUAS. *See* Figure 5-6. Such records should include all components of the sUAS, including the:

- Small unmanned aircraft itself;
- Control station;
- Launch and recovery equipment;
- Data link equipment;
- Payload; and
- Any other components required to safely operate the sUAS.

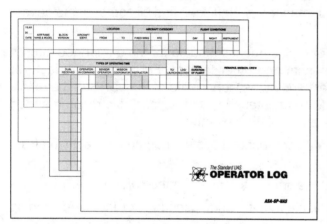

Figure 5-6. A UAS logbook can be used to track remote pilot hours as well as sUAS maintenance

1265. Which of the following sources of information should you consult first when determining what maintenance should be performed on an sUAS or its components?

A— Local pilot best practices.
B— 14 CFR Part 107.
C— Manufacturer guidance.

The preferred source of information is the manufacturer's guidance about maintenance schedule and instructions. (PLT439) — AC 107-2

1266. Under what condition should the operator of a small unmanned aircraft establish a scheduled maintenance protocol?

A— When the manufacturer does not provide a maintenance schedule.
B— When the FAA requires you to, following an accident.
C— Small unmanned aircraft systems do not require maintenance.

Follow all manufacturer maintenance recommendations to achieve the longest and safest service life of the sUAS. If the sUAS or component manufacturer does not provide scheduled maintenance instructions, it is recommended that you establish your own scheduled maintenance protocol. (PLT446) — AC 107-2

1267. Scheduled maintenance should be performed in accordance with the

A— Manufacturer's suggested procedures.
B— Stipulations in 14 CFR Part 43.
C— Contractor requirements.

Follow all manufacturer maintenance recommendations to achieve the longest and safest service life of the sUAS. If the sUAS or component manufacturer does not provide scheduled maintenance instructions, it is recommended that you establish your own scheduled maintenance protocol. (PLT446) — AC 107-2

Answers

1265 [C]   1266 [A]   1267 [A]

1268. The responsibility for ensuring that an sUAS is maintained in an airworthy condition is primarily that of the

A— Remote pilot in command.
B— owner or operator.
C— mechanic who performs the work.

No person may operate a sUAS unless it is in a condition for safe operation. Prior to each flight, the remote PIC must check the sUAS to determine whether it is in a condition for safe operation. No person may continue flight of the small unmanned aircraft when he or she knows or has reason to know that the small unmanned aircraft system is no longer in a condition for safe operation. (PLT374) — 14 CFR §107.15

1269. When should the battery for an unmanned aircraft be replaced?

A— Once recharged more than 10 times in the preceding 30 days.
B— Per the guidelines of the sUAS manufacturer or the battery manufacturer, whichever is more restrictive.
C— Per the guidelines of the sUAS manufacturer or the battery manufacturer, whichever is least restrictive.

Follow all manufacturer maintenance recommendations to achieve the longest and safest service life of the sUAS. By abiding by the more restrictive limitation or component life cycle, the remote PIC will be assured of being in compliance of both the sUAS and battery manufacturers' guidelines. (PLT446) — AC 107-2

Answers

1268 [A]   1269 [B]

The following list of the numbered questions included in this ASA Test Prep is given in sequential order; however, as a result of our ongoing review of FAA test question databases, some question numbers may have been removed due to changes in the database. **All currently existing questions are accounted for in this list.** For more information about the questions included in ASA Test Preps, please read Pages v–vi in the front matter for this book.

Question Number	Page Number	Question Number	Page Number	Question Number	Page Number	Question Number	Page Number
1001	1–4	1040	1–16	1079	2–10	1118	2–22
1002	1–4	1041	1–17	1080	2–10	1119	2–22
1003	1–4	1042	1–17	1081	2–10	1120	2–22
1004	1–4	1043	1–18	1082	2–10	1121	2–23
1005	1–5	1044	1–18	1083	2–10	1122	2–23
1006	1–5	1045	1–18	1084	2–10	1123	2–23
1007	1–5	1046	1–18	1085	2–11	1124	2–23
1008	1–5	1047	1–19	1086	2–12	1125	2–23
1009	1–5	1048	1–19	1087	2–12	1126	2–23
1010	1–5	1049	1–19	1088	2–12	1128	2–24
1011	1–5	1050	1–20	1089	2–12	1129	2–24
1012	1–7	1051	1–20	1090	2–12	1130	2–26
1013	1–7	1052	1–20	1091	2–12	1131	2–26
1014	1–7	1053	1–21	1092	2–13	1132	2–26
1015	1–7	1054	1–21	1093	2–13	1133	2–26
1016	1–8	1055	1–22	1094	2–13	1134	2–26
1017	1–8	1056	1–23	1095	2–13	1135	3–3
1018	1–8	1057	1–23	1096	2–14	1136	3–3
1019	1–8	1058	1–23	1097	2–15	1137	3–4
1020	1–9	1059	1–24	1098	2–15	1138	3–4
1021	1–10	1060	1–24	1099	2–15	1139	3–4
1022	1–10	1061	1–24	1100	2–15	1140	3–5
1023	1–10	1062	1–24	1101	2–15	1141	3–5
1024	1–10	1063	1–24	1102	2–15	1142	3–6
1025	1–10	1064	1–25	1103	2–16	1143	3–6
1026	1–11	1065	1–26	1104	2–16	1144	3–6
1027	1–12	1066	1–26	1105	2–16	1145	3–7
1028	1–12	1067	2–4	1106	2–16	1146	3–7
1029	1–12	1068	2–4	1107	2–16	1147	3–7
1030	1–12	1069	2–5	1108	2–17	1148	3–8
1031	1–13	1070	2–5	1109	2–17	1149	3–8
1032	1–13	1071	2–5	1110	2–17	1150	3–8
1033	1–14	1072	2–5	1111	2–19	1151	3–9
1034	1–14	1073	2–5	1112	2–19	1152	3–9
1035	1–14	1074	2–6	1113	2–19	1153	3–11
1036	1–15	1075	2–6	1114	2–19	1154	3–11
1037	1–15	1076	2–6	1115	2–19	1155	3–11
1038	1–15	1077	2–9	1116	2–22	1156	3–11
1039	1–16	1078	2–9	1117	2–22	1157	3–11

Appendix B
Learning Statement Code and Question Number

The expression "learning statement," as used in FAA airman testing, refers to measurable statements about the knowledge a student should be able to demonstrate following certain segments of training. When you take the applicable airman knowledge test required for an airman pilot certificate or rating, you will receive an Airman Knowledge Test Report. The test report will list the learning statement codes for questions you have answered incorrectly. Match the codes given on your test report to the ones listed in this cross-reference. Use Appendix A in this book to find the page number for the question numbers listed below.

The FAA sample questions for the Unmanned Aircraft General—Small (UAG) test shows two types of codes associated with each question:

- The Learning Statement Code(s) (LSCs) associated with the question topic areas. The LSC codes currently appear on the Airman Knowledge Test Report for any missed knowledge test questions.

- The Airman Certification Standards (ACS) code for the question topic area. The FAA expects the ACS codes to replace the LSC codes on the UAG knowledge test report within the next 12-18 months.

You can view the complete list of LSCs used on this test in the *Remote Pilot Test Guide* (FAA-G-8082-20), posted on the Reader Resource page **www.asa2fly.com/reader/TPUAS**. If you received a code on your Airman Test Report that is not listed in this cross-reference, email ASA at **cfi@asa2fly.com**. We will provide the definition so you can review that subject area.

The FAA appreciates testing experience feedback. You can contact the branch responsible for the FAA Knowledge Exams directly at:

Federal Aviation Administration
AFS-630 Airman Testing Standards Branch
PO Box 25082
Oklahoma City, OK 73125
Email: afs630comments@faa.gov

Learning Statement Code	FAA Reference	Subject Description & Question Numbers
PLT015	FAA-H-8083-25	Calculate flight performance, planning, range *1208*
PLT018	FAA-H-8083-25	Calculate load factor, stall speed, velocity, angle of attack *1196, 1197, 1198*
PLT026	FAA-H-8083-25	Define ceiling *1300*
PLT040	AIM	Interpret airspace classes: charts, diagrams *1077, 1078, 1082, 1083, 1084, 1085, 1093, 1094, 1282, 1296, 1309*
PLT044	AIM	Interpret ATC communications, instructions, terminology *1227*
PLT059	AC 00-45	Interpret information on a METAR/SPECI report *1180, 1181, 1292*
PLT064	AIM, Sectional Chart Legend, 14 CFR Part 107	Interpret information on a Sectional Chart *1088, 1090, 1092, 1096, 1097, 1098, 1099, 1100, 1101, 1102, 1103, 1104, 1105, 1106, 1107, 1108, 1109, 1110, 1111, 1139, 1188, 1224, 1284, 1295, 1301, 1305, 1307,*
PLT072	AC 00-45	Interpret information on a TAF 1182, 1183, 1184, 1185
PLT098	FAA-H-8083-25	Recall aeromedical factors: fitness for flight *1254, 1262*
PLT101	FAA-H-8083-25	Recall aeronautical charts: pilotage *1089*
PLT103	FAA-H-8083-25	Recall ADM, hazardous attitudes *1246, 1247, 1248, 1249, 1291*
PLT104	AC 107-2	Recall ADM, human factors, CRM *1242, 1243, 1244, 1250, 1251, 1252, 1253, 1299, 1315*
PLT116	AIM	Recall aircraft general knowledge, publications, AIM, navigational aids *1074, 1128*
PLT119	14 CFR Part 107	Regulations: aircraft lighting *1039*
PLT124	AC 00-6	Recall aircraft performance: atmospheric effects *1290*
PLT127	FAA-H-8083-25	Recall aircraft performance: density altitude *1173, 1174*
PLT129	FAA-H-8083-25	Recall aircraft performance: effects of runway slope, slope landing *1206*
PLT130	FAA-H-8083-25	Recall aircraft performance: fuel *1209*

Learning Statement Code	FAA Reference	Subject Description & Question Numbers
PLT134	FAA-H-8083-25	Recall aircraft performance: takeoff *1207*
PLT141	AIM	Recall airport operations: markings, signs, lighting *1116, 1121, 1122, 1123, 1124, 1125, 1126, 1127, 1129*
PLT146	AIM	Recall airport operations: traffic pattern procedures, communication procedures *1112, 1113, 1114, 1117, 1118, 1119, 1120, 1217, 1218, 1219, 1220, 1221, 1222, 1225, 1228, 1229, 1230, 1231, 1232, 1233, 1308*
PLT161	*Chart Supplement U.S.*	Recall airspace classes: limits, requirements, restrictions, airspeeds, equipment *1075, 1079, 1080, 1081*
PLT163	14 CFR Part 107	Recall airspace requirements: visibility, cloud clearance *1151, 1152, 1271, 1288, 1289, 1310*
PLT168	FAA-H-8083-25	Recall angle of attack: characteristics, forces, principles *1201, 1202*
PLT173	AC 00-6	Recall atmospheric conditions: measurements, pressure, stability *1137, 1148, 1149*
PLT192	AC 00-6	Recall clouds: types/formation/resulting weather *1278, 1283, 1287*
PLT194	AIM	Recall collision avoidance, scanning techniques *1131, 1132, 1133, 1134, 1303*
PLT196	AIM	Recall communications: ATIS broadcasts *1223, 1226, 1279*
PLT198	FAA-H-8083-25	Recall course/heading: effects of wind *1140, 1141*
PLT200	FAA-H-8083-25, AC 107-2	Recall dead reckoning: calculations, charts *1187*
PLT205	AIM	Recall effects of alcohol on the body *1062, 1302*
PLT206	AC 00-6	Recall effects of temperature: density altitude, icing *1176*
PLT208	SAFO 10017, AC 107-2, 14 CFR Part 107	Recall emergency conditions, procedures *1234, 1235, 1236, 1237, 1238, 1239, 1240, 1241*
PLT220	14 CFR Part 107	Regulations: night operations *1040, 1274*
PLT222	FAA-H-8083-25	Recall aircraft operations: checklist usage *1210*

Learning Statement Code	FAA Reference	Subject Description & Question Numbers
PLT226	AC 00-6	Recall fog: types, formation, resulting weather *1167, 1168, 1169, 1170, 1171, 1172*
PLT242	FAA-H-8083-1	Recall forces acting on aircraft: lift, drag, thrust, weight, stall, limitations *1193, 1194*
PLT263	AC 00-6	Recall hazardous weather: fog, icing, turbulence, visibility restriction *1164, 1165, 1166*
PLT271	FAA-H-8083-25	Recall human factors (ADM) judgment *1245*
PLT272	FAA-H-8083-25	Recall human factors, stress management *1255, 1256, 1257, 1258, 1297*
PLT281	FAA-H-8083-25	Recall information in *Chart Supplement U.S.* *1067, 1076*
PLT290	AC 00-45	Recall information on AIRMETs/SIGMETs *1311*
PLT301	AC 00-6	Recall inversion layer: characteristics *1285*
PLT310	FAA-H-8083-25	Recall load factor: characteristics *1195, 1199, 1200, 1204*
PLT312	FAA-H-8083-3	Recall load factor: maneuvering, stall speed *1203, 1293*
PLT313	AC 107-2	Recall loading: limitations, terminology *1190, 1191, 1192*
PLT323	FAA-H-8083-25	Recall NOTAMs: classes, information, distribution *1068, 1069, 1070, 1071, 1276, 1313*
PLT328	FAA-H-8083-25	Recall performance planning: aircraft loading *1314*
PLT332	AIM	Recall physiological factors: hyperventilation *1259, 1273, 1260*
PLT333	FAA-H-8083-25, 14 CFR Part 107	Recall physiological factors: night vision *1263, 1264*
PLT345	FAA-H-8083-25	Recall pressure altitude *1175, 1272, 1277, 1286, 1298*
PLT351	FAA-H-8083-25	Recall propeller system: types, components, operating principles, characteristics *1177*
PLT366	14 CFR Part 107	Regulations: accident/incident reporting and preserving wreckage *1027, 1028, 1029, 1030*

Learning Statement Code	FAA Reference	Subject Description & Question Numbers
PLT372	14 CFR Part 107	Regulations: aircraft inspection, records, expiration *1036*
PLT373	14 CFR Part 107	Regulations: aircraft operating limitations *1020, 1021, 1022, 1041, 1042, 1043, 1044, 1045, 1050, 1051, 1052, 1053, 1054, 1055, 1065, 1066, 1270*
PLT374	14 CFR Part 107	Recall regulations: aircraft owner/operator responsibilities *1268*
PLT376	FAA-H-8083-25	Regulations: airspace special use, TFRs *1072, 1073, 1086, 1087, 1095*
PLT387	14 CFR Part 107	Regulations: change of address *1064*
PLT395	14 CFR Part 107, AC 107-2	Regulations: definitions *1004, 1005*
PLT401	AC 107-2	Regulations: dropping, aerial application, towing restrictions *1056, 1057, 1058*
PLT403	14 CFR Part 107	Regulations: emergency deviation from regulations *1009, 1010, 1011*
PLT405	AC 107-2	Regulations: equipment, instrument, certificate requirements *1038*
PLT414	14 CFR Part 107	Regulations: general right-of-way rules *1047, 1048, 1049, 1091, 1312*
PLT427	14 CFR Part 107	Regulations: medical certificate requirements, validity *1014, 1015*
PLT430	AC 107-2	Recall regulations: minimum safe, flight altitude *1189*
PLT439	AC 107-2	Recall regulations: persons authorized to perform maintenance *1265*
PLT440	14 CFR Part 107	Regulations: pilot/crew duties and responsibilities *1016, 1017, 1023, 1024, 1025*
PLT441	14 CFR Part 107, AC 107-2	Regulations: pilot briefing *1019*
PLT442	14 CFR Part 107	Regulations: pilot currency requirements *1013, 1304*
PLT443	14 CFR Part 107	Regulations: pilot qualifications, privileges, responsibilities, crew complement *1001, 1018*
PLT444	14 CFR Part 107	Regulations: pilot-in-command authority, responsibility *1008*

Learning Statement Code	FAA Reference	Subject Description & Question Numbers
PLT445	14 CFR Part 107	Regulations: preflight requirements *1037, 1186, 1211, 1212, 1213, 1214, 1215, 1216*
PLT446	AC 107-2	Recall regulations: preventative maintenance *1266, 1267, 1269*
PLT448	14 CFR Part 107	Regulations: privileges, limitations of pilot certificates *1002, 1003, 1006, 1007, 1012, 1031, 1032*
PLT454	14 CFR Part 107	Regulations: required aircraft, equipment inspections *1026, 1205*
PLT463	14 CFR Part 107	Regulations: alcohol or drugs *1059, 1060, 1061, 1063, 1261, 1275, 1306*
PLT494	AC 00-6	Recall thermals: types, characteristics, formation, locating, hazards, precipitation static *1138*
PLT495	AC 00-6	Recall thunderstorms: types, characteristics, formation, hazards, precipitation static *1153, 1154, 1155, 1156, 1157, 1158, 1159, 1160, 1161, 1162, 1163*
PLT498	49 CFR Part 1544	Recall Transportation Security Regulations *1115*
PLT510	AC 107-2	Recall weather: causes, formation *1135, 1136*
PLT511	AC 0-6	Recall weather associated with frontal activity, air masses *1142, 1143, 1144, 1145, 1146, 1147, 1150*
PLT514	FAA-H-8083-25	Recall weather reporting systems: briefings, forecasts, reports, AWOS/ASOS *1178, 1179*
PLT526	FAA-H-8083-25	Recall near midair collision report *1130*
PLT527	14 CFR Part 107	Regulations: basic VFR weather minimums *1046*
PLT528	14 CFR Part 107	Recall regulations: small UAS operations/weight limitations *1280*
PLT529	FAA-H-8083-25	Recall physiological factors: prescription and over-the-counter drugs *1281*
PLT530	14 CFR Part 107	Regulations: registration requirements for small unmanned aircraft systems *1033, 1034, 1035*

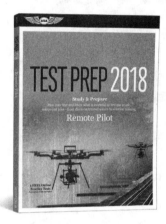

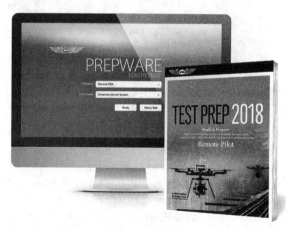

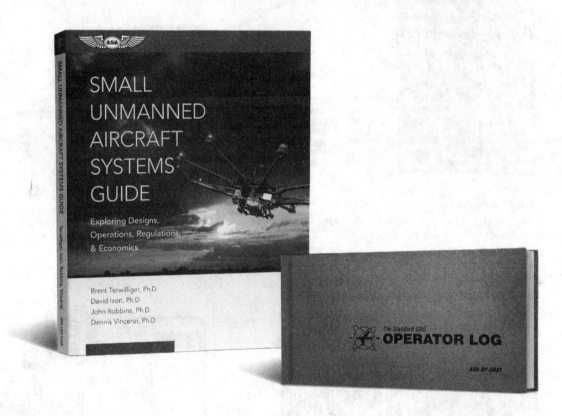